True Stories of Teens in the Holocaust

YOUTH DESTROYED— THE NAZI CAMPS

PRIMARY SOURCES FROM THE HOLOCAUST

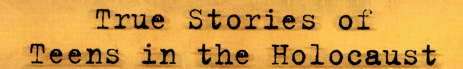

Other Titles in the
True Stories of Teens in the Holocaust
Series

COURAGEOUS TEEN RESISTERS
PRIMARY SOURCES FROM THE HOLOCAUST
ISBN-13: 978-0-7660-3269-9

ESCAPE—TEENS ON THE RUN
PRIMARY SOURCES FROM THE HOLOCAUST
ISBN-13: 978-0-7660-3270-5

HIDDEN TEENS, HIDDEN LIVES
PRIMARY SOURCES FROM THE HOLOCAUST
ISBN-13: 978-0-7660-3271-2

SHATTERED YOUTH IN NAZI GERMANY
PRIMARY SOURCES FROM THE HOLOCAUST
ISBN-13: 978-0-7660-3268-2

TRAPPED—YOUTH IN THE NAZI GHETTOS
PRIMARY SOURCES FROM THE HOLOCAUST
ISBN-13: 978-0-7660-3272-9

True Stories of Teens in the Holocaust

YOUTH DESTROYED— THE NAZI CAMPS

PRIMARY SOURCES FROM THE HOLOCAUST

Ann Byers

Holocaust research by
Margaret Shannon,
*Senior Research Historian,
Washington Historical Research*

Enslow Publishers, Inc.
40 Industrial Road
Box 398
Berkeley Heights, NJ 07922
USA
http://www.enslow.com

Copyright © 2010 by Enslow Publishers, Inc.

All rights reserved.

No part of this book may be reproduced by any means without the written permission of the publisher.

Library of Congress Cataloging-in-Publication Data

Byers, Ann.
   Youth destroyed—the Nazi camps : primary sources from the Holocaust / Ann Byers.
     p. cm. — (True stories of teens in the Holocaust)
   Includes bibliographical references and index.
   Summary: "Discusses the experiences of children and teens in concentration camps during the Holocaust, including the first camps in Germany, the forced labor camps, the six death camps, and the aftermath"—Provided by publisher.
   ISBN-13: 978-0-7660-3273-6
   ISBN-10: 0-7660-3273-6
   1. Jewish children in the Holocaust—Biography—Juvenile literature. 2. World War, 1939–1945—Concentration camps—Juvenile literature. 3. World War, 1939–1945—Children—Juvenile literature. 4. Holocaust, Jewish (1939–1945)—Juvenile literature. I. Title.
   D804.48.B948 2010
   940.53'18083—dc22
                                                                  2009026167

Printed in the United States of America

042011 Lake Book Manufacturing, Inc., Melrose Park, IL

10 9 8 7 6 5 4 3 2

To Our Readers: We have done our best to make sure all Internet Addresses in this book were active and appropriate when we went to press. However, the author and the publisher have no control over and assume no liability for the material available on those Internet sites or on other Web sites they may link to. Any comments or suggestions can be sent by e-mail to comments@enslow.com or to the address on the back cover.

Every effort has been made to locate all copyright holders of material used in this book. If any errors or omissions have occurred, please contact us at www.enslow.com. We will try to make corrections in future editions.

Enslow Publishers, Inc., is committed to printing our books on recycled paper. The paper in every book contains 10% to 30% post-consumer waste (PCW). The cover board on the outside of each book contains 100% PCW. Our goal is to do our part to help young people and the environment too!

Illustration Credits: Associated Press, p. 52; Enslow Publishers, Inc., p. 26; ullstein bild / The Granger Collection, New York, p. 24; USHMM, pp. 17, 111; USHMM, courtesy of Anonymous Donor, pp. 83, 113; USHMM, courtesy of Archiv der KZ-Gedenkstaette Mauthausen, pp. 56, 112; USHMM, courtesy of Archiwum Panstwowego Muzeum na Majdanku, p. 76; USHMM, courtesy of Belarussian State Archive of Documentary Film and Photography, pp. 97, 113; USHMM, courtesy of Bruce Tapper, p. 14; USHMM, courtesy of Central State Archive of Documentary Film and Photography, p. 49; USHMM, courtesy of Dana Upton, p. 101; USHMM, courtesy of Dora Rubinsztejn Weiner, p. 34; USHMM, courtesy of Edgar and Hana Krasa, pp. 1, 3, 86, 113; USHMM, courtesy of Eva Tuchsznajder Lang, pp. 31, 111; USHMM, courtesy of Frieda Fisz Greenspan, p. 91; USHMM, courtesy of Hedwig Wachenheimer Epstein, pp. 19, 111; USHMM, courtesy of Helen Waterford, p. 44; USHMM, courtesy of Instytut Pamieci Nardowej, pp. 46, 88; USHMM, courtesy of KZ Gedenkstaette Dachau, p. 22; USHMM, courtesy of Leo Bretholz, pp. 37, 112; USHMM, courtesy of Lev Sviridov, p. 11; USHMM, courtesy of Lilly Lax Friedman, p. 107; USHMM, courtesy of Lilo Plaschkes, pp. 105, 113; USHMM, courtesy of Michael (Fink) Barak, pp. 39, 112; USHMM, courtesy of Muzeum Regionalne with Tomaszow Lubelski, pp. 69, 112; USHMM, courtesy of National Archives and Records Administration, pp. 61, 103; USHMM, courtesy of Panstwowe Muzeum with Oswiecim-Brzezinka, p. 80; USHMM, courtesy of Peter Feigl, pp. 28–29; USHMM, courtesy of Polskie Koleje Panstwowe S.A., p. 72; USHMM, courtesy of Sheva Zilberg, p. 65; USHMM, courtesy of Yad Vashem, pp. 8, 10, 111.

Cover Illustration: USHMM, courtesy of Edgar and Hana Krasa (Face of Edgar Krasa in a photo taken circa 1940–1941, a survivor of a few Nazi camps, including Auschwitz).

Contents

	Acknowledgments	6
	Introduction	7
Chapter 1	**The Concentration Camps**	13
Chapter 2	**Waiting Rooms**	27
Chapter 3	**Worked to Death**	42
Chapter 4	**The Death Camps**	59
Chapter 5	**Auschwitz**	78
Chapter 6	**After the Camps**	93
	Chart of Camp Deaths	110
	Timeline	111
	Chapter Notes	114
	Glossary	122
	Further Reading	124
	Internet Addresses	125
	Index	126

Acknowledgments

Special thanks to the people of the United States Holocaust Memorial Museum in Washington, D.C., for all their help in completing this book.

Introduction

Alice Lok was barely fifteen when she arrived at Auschwitz. By the time she came to this place—the largest of all the Nazi camps—hundreds of thousands had met their deaths there. She arrived in the summer of 1944, one of more than four hundred thousand Jews transported from Hungary to the huge complex in Poland.

Auschwitz had been in operation since 1940, shortly after Adolf Hitler, the leader of Nazi Germany, began World War II. At that time, it was a concentration camp. But two years later, the first of four gas chambers was built on the grounds. More than one million people were killed in the gas chambers and their bodies burned to ashes in the crematoria connected to them. Auschwitz was a tool of the Holocaust: Adolf Hitler and the Nazi's attempt to rid Europe of all its Jews.

Alice Lok was almost one of Hitler's victims. When new people entered the camp, they were met by a Nazi doctor who directed them to one of two lines. This process was called a "selection." The people who could work, who were considered useful to the Nazis, went in one line; everyone else was pointed to the line that went directly to the gas chambers. Young children almost always were in the death line. The guard who decided Lok's fate was a woman:

YOUTH DESTROYED—THE NAZI CAMPS

Jews from a large transport stand in line for selection at Auschwitz in May 1944. Alice Lok had to go through such a selection when she arrived at Auschwitz.

INTRODUCTION

"There," she motioned as I stepped naked and shivering in front of her. With the motion of her hand she would decide if I should live or be sent to the crematorium.

I stretched my frail body to impress her with my youthful strength and, looking straight into her eyes, I whispered: "It's my fifteenth birthday today."

Our eyes met for a moment. She hesitated, then her hand shifted directions. "There," she said loudly. Her voice filled with annoyance for the delay—it just took seconds.

I looked around. Hundreds of people, faceless in their haunted bodies, assembled toward the other direction. My pencil-thin legs quivered like wheat in a breezy day. "Freedom! Freedom! God granted me freedom."[1]

Lok's "freedom" did not last long. Every day prisoners in the work camps of Auschwitz were selected for the gas chambers. Lok's turn came on October 7, 1944. As she and other children stood in line awaiting their fate, she heard an explosion. A group of inmates had rebelled, setting fire to one of the crematoria. In the commotion that followed, Lok and the others were ordered back to their barracks.

A month after the surprise rebellion that saved Lok's life, the Nazis dismantled Auschwitz's gas chambers. Germany was losing the war, and the Nazis did not want the death camps discovered. The prisoners were marched to camps farther away from the battle lines in January 1945. Lok went to Guben, a subcamp of Gross-Rosen in Germany.

Jewish women and children who have been selected for death walk toward the gas chambers in Auschwitz. Alice Lok was saved from the gas chambers on October 7, 1944, when some inmates in Auschwitz started a rebellion.

She refused to let the harsh conditions of a work camp and the ever-present fear of death rob her of all hope. At Guben, guards commanded the children to decorate their barracks for Christmas. Lok used the opportunity to defy the Nazis by proudly displaying her faith:

> There were no paper or pencils to make decorations; we practically had nothing except one broom to sweep the floor with. We were about 24 children in our barrack. I decided we should choreograph ourselves into a living candelabra [a Jewish symbol for Hanukkah] and hold the pieces of the broom as a part of this sculpture. We won a prize—each of us a little can of snails.[2]

INTRODUCTION

Lok did not stay in Guben for long. As Germany's enemies advanced toward the camp, the Nazis marched its inmates to prisons deeper in Germany. Lok found her new home even worse than the previous camps:

> Bergen-Belsen was hell on earth. Nothing ever in literature could compare to anything that Bergen-Belsen was. When we arrived, the dead were not carried away any more. You stepped over them. You fell over them if you couldn't walk. There were agonizing . . . people begging for water. They were . . . falling into planks that were not pulled together in the barracks.

Alice Lok called Bergen-Belsen "hell on earth." These surviving prisoners stand behind the fence at Bergen-Belsen in April 1945.

> They were crying, they were begging. . . .
> It was hell. Day and night. You couldn't
> escape the crying, you couldn't have
> escaped the praying. You couldn't escape
> the [cries of] "Mercy!" It was a chant, the
> chant of the dead. It was hell.[3]

For Lok, the hell lasted several months. She was one of the lucky ones, still alive when British soldiers liberated the camp in April 1945. At sixteen, she had survived while other members of her family had not. She had lived through two brutal work camps and Auschwitz—the most infamous of all the death camps. Twelve million others were not so fortunate; that is one estimate of the number of people killed during the Holocaust.[4] Six million were Jews and 1.5 million were children.

Some were killed by soldiers and others sweeping through their cities, looking for Jews. Some died of starvation and mistreatment in crowded ghettos of cities the Nazis controlled. At least 3 million Jews perished in the twenty thousand camps of the Holocaust.

Chapter One

THE CONCENTRATION CAMPS

The Holocaust camps that claimed so many lives did not begin as death camps. Hitler built them as prisons for his political opponents. They were not made for Jews, but for enemies of the German government. However, Adolf Hitler considered Jews enemies of Nazi Germany. He was fanatically antisemitic—prejudiced against Jews.

Antisemitism was not new in the 1930s. Over the centuries, at various times and places, people persecuted Jews for no reason other than that they were Jews. In the early twentieth century, prejudice against Jews was strong in many parts of Europe, especially in Russia and Poland. But despite the intolerance, Jewish people thrived and contributed to their communities.

As the Nazi Party in Germany rose in influence in the 1930s, the position of Jews began to change. Golly D., eleven when Hitler became chancellor (leader) of Germany in 1933, had long experienced antisemitism in her home in Bremen. However, it did not bother her much:

> In the early twenties the Brown Shirts [members of Hitler's military-like organization] started marching through the streets singing antisemitic songs, which somehow didn't faze us all that much because we lived in our own little world. I never felt at that point in time that I was

Despite the antisemitism in Europe, Jewish people had built strong and flourishing communities, especially in eastern Europe. The exterior of a synagogue in Katowice, Poland, is shown on this postcard from the early 1900s.

> discriminated against. And so it went until Hitler came to power in January 1933.[1]

When Hitler took charge, he immediately set about making laws that singled out Jews. Jews could not be treated in government hospitals, they could not hold jobs as doctors or lawyers, and they were banned from parks and libraries, among many other restrictions. Golly felt the sting of the stronger antisemitism:

> We were not permitted to have any social contact with non-Jews. . . . One day . . . a childhood friend, a youth friend, came to pick me up from school after school was out. We . . . were about halfway home and

> were suddenly stopped by a Gestapo [Nazi
> police] agent. . . . He approached this
> young boy. . . . He argued with him severely.
> He made his father appear at Gestapo
> headquarters and threatened the father that
> if his son would ever be seen again with a
> Jew or Jewess, he and the son would end up
> in a concentration camp.[2]

The threat of ending up in a camp struck fear in the hearts of many Germans. The camps were dreadful places. They were called concentration camps because prisoners were concentrated, or gathered, in one place. The purpose of the camps was to intimidate Hitler's enemies. The Nazis tried to frighten their opponents into doing what they wanted. If they could not scare them, they tortured them into submission.

Generally, the Jews were not political opponents of the government. So for more than five and a half years after the first camp was opened, Jews were not interned in large numbers at the camps. That changed suddenly, in one terrible night.

Kristallnacht

On the night of November 9, 1938, an event occurred that became known as *Kristallnacht*, the Night of Broken Glass. Just two days earlier, a seventeen-year-old Jew shot and killed Ernst vom Rath, a minor German official, outside the German Embassy in Paris, France. The young man, Herschel Grynszpan, was angry because Hitler had expelled his family and more than twelve thousand other Jews from Germany. They were left at the Polish border with no place to go. The Nazis used the assassination as an excuse to rally people to violence against Jews. In hundreds of cities and towns throughout Germany and Austria, angry mobs of Nazis attacked Jewish businesses, homes, and synagogues (Jewish place of worship). As police and firefighters looked on, the lawless crowds shattered windows, burned buildings, and killed Jews.

Seventeen-year-old Vera Dahl saw the destruction from the window of a bus in the city of Aachen: "We . . . passed various Jewish shops . . . all windows broken or smashed, glass everywhere. . . . Shops were being looted as we passed. I was petrified."[3]

Not only Jewish stores, but also their houses were destroyed. Rita Braumann turned twelve years old the day the Nazis came to her home in Cologne. She listened as they ransacked her family's belongings:

> The noise was terrifying. . . . Absolutely everything had been demolished. Shattered glass made it dangerous to walk anywhere. Bottles of wine had been poured over Persian carpets, home-made jam had been emptied all over the place. . . . Valuable paintings had been slashed with an axe or knives.[4]

Not content to destroy property, the Nazis murdered ninety-one Jews on the Night of Broken Glass. Fourteen-year-old Laurie Lowenthal was asleep in his home in Aschaffenburg when the chaos erupted:

> We were woken by the sound of shooting. My father's cousin . . . lived on the first floor of our house with his family. Two men broke down their front door and shot him point blank while he was in bed. . . . Meanwhile, his brother-in-law . . . was

THE CONCENTRATION CAMPS

These Torah scrolls were desecrated during Kristallnacht. The Nazis unleashed a wave of destruction during the violent attack.

kidnapped, taken to the nearby woods, tied to a tree and used as target practice.[5]

Many who were not killed were sent to concentration camps. During the twenty-four-hour rampage, more than thirty thousand Jewish men between sixteen and sixty years of age were arrested and interned in camps. Lea Weems was only six on Kristallnacht, but she recalled vividly the night her father was taken:

> Three Nazis . . . were carrying axes, hammers and saws. They pushed us aside and began to destroy everything in our house. . . . When everything was broken, they pushed my father and my grandfather down the stairs. I was screaming and pulling on my father's sleeve trying to keep him from leaving. I saw a row of men standing in the street—they had been arrested—and my father and grandfather were taken away with the others. . . . I learned later that the men were taken to Dachau.[6]

Concentration Camps

Dachau was the first major concentration camp. But it was not the only one. By the Night of Broken Glass, the internment camps of Sachsenhausen, Buchenwald, and Flossenbürg were already operating in Germany, and Mauthausen was open in Austria. (Germany took over Austria in March 1938.) The thirty thousand arrested that night were taken to these camps. Fourteen-year-old Hedy Epstein watched with a classmate from their school's window in the town of Kippenheim:

THE CONCENTRATION CAMPS

```
What we saw were men being marched down
the street, four in a row, accompanied by
SS men who were hitting them with whips
and urging them to walk faster. . . .
The feeling was just indescribable: fear,
anger, frustration, wanting to do something
and not knowing what to do.⁷
```

Conditions in the concentration camps were harsh. Theodore Haas, twenty-one when arrested during Kristallnacht, knew that people "used to frighten their children [by telling them], 'If you do not behave, you will surely end up at Dachau.'"⁸ Haas lived three years in Dachau and found it far worse than he imagined:

Hedy Epstein watched from her window as men were marched down the street to concentration camps. Hedy is pictured with a white bow sitting next to her grandmother in this group portrait taken in August 1937.

19

YOUTH DESTROYED—THE NAZI CAMPS

> We were issued one quarter of a loaf of bread . . . to last three days. In the morning, we picked up, at the kitchen, a cup of roasted barley drink. There was no lunch. At dinnertime, sometimes we got a watery soup. . . . We were forced to sleep on straw. As time went on, the straw disintegrated and we became louse infested. The guards delighted in making weak and ill clothed prisoners march or stand at attention in rain, snow, and ice for hours. As you can imagine, death came often due to the conditions. . . . [Sometimes] a guard or a group of them would single out a prisoner and beat him with canes or a club. Sometimes to further terrorize a prisoner, the guards would form a circle around a prisoner and beat him unconscious. . . . Three times a day, we were counted. We had to carry the dead to the square. Each time, we had to stand at attention in all kinds of weather. We stood wearing next to nothing . . . while our tormentors had sheepskin coats and felt boots.[9]

Life in the concentration camps was brutal, but the prisoners were eventually released. The typical stay was about a year, although some, like Haas, were held as long as three years. Even the thousands of Jews interned after Kristallnacht were eventually let out—on the condition that they would leave Germany.

Not everyone came back from the prisons. Thirteen-year-old Ursula Rosenfeld's father did not return. When other prisoners came back to her little town of Quackenbrück, she learned what happened to her father:

> When they came to Buchenwald and they took
> away all the men's braces and shoelaces,
> [my father] protested and said, "You can't
> treat these old people like this." So they
> made an example of him and they beat him
> to death in front of everybody in order to
> instill terror and obedience. We heard a
> few days later that he had died of a heart
> attack, but this was the story the Nazis
> told all the families of the people they
> killed.[10]

Once war started, almost no one returned from the camps. The Nazis issued an order that prisoners were not to be released until the war was over. In fact, World War II brought dramatic changes to the entire camp system.

World War II

On September 1, 1939, Hitler's army invaded Poland, beginning what would become known as the Second World War. Seven months later, German armies occupied Denmark and Norway. The next month they marched into Belgium, Luxembourg, France, and the Netherlands. By June 1941, much of western Europe was under German control and Hitler's army was poised to attack the Soviet Union to the east.

Every new conquest brought more prisoners to the concentration camps. The camps had to be enlarged, and new ones needed to be built. Prisoner-of-war (POW) camps were constructed to hold captured soldiers.

German victories opened up areas beyond Germany's borders where new camps could be located: Natzweiler, France; Danica,

Inmates at the Dachau concentration camp gather outside to hear a speech by Hitler in 1934. Initially, Dachau imprisoned only German political enemies. However, after Kristallnacht, it began to detain large numbers of Jews.

Croatia (Yugoslavia); and Auschwitz, Poland. The very first camp outside Germany was built at Stutthof near Danzig (now Gdansk, Poland). Twenty-two-year-old Leo Kutner was arrested in Danzig on the first day of the war and was eventually placed in Stutthof. He described it as a horrible place:

> There were very, very harsh conditions. SS [guards were] standing all around the camp. And they would not only beat you and abuse you, but if they felt like it, they would grab [your] . . . head covering and throw it and say, "Mach schnell [Fast!]—hurry up . . . get your cap." And as you went to get

> your cap they would shoot you. And then
> they would write down on the report, "Shot
> while trying to escape."[11]

In addition to creating a need for more camps, the war required more workers than Germany could produce. Someone had to manufacture the weapons, sew the uniforms, and grow the food for the army. The camps had a growing supply of able-bodied men and women. After the war started, the concentration camps were converted from prison camps to forced labor camps. Their purpose shifted from political detention to economic production. Bela Blau, a Slovakian Jew interned in Mauthausen, was forced to repair the weapons of his enemy:

> From Mauthausen, we were taken over to
> Gusen [a subcamp of Mauthausen], which
> [was] an ammunition factory, partly. . . .
> One of the factories was the Messerschmitt
> Werke, for the Messerschmitt planes—war
> planes. So I was assigned . . . to fix the
> petrol tanks, the gas tanks, in the wings
> of the Messerschmitt.[12]

The "Final Solution"

The war also gave the Nazis an opportunity to finally "solve" the "Jewish problem." In anticipation of a "solution," a year before the war started, they had expelled all Jews of Polish descent from Germany. Alexander Gordon was sixteen on October 28, 1938, when a train came to Hamburg for that purpose:

> We were suddenly summoned . . . and
> everybody lined up . . . boys and girls.
> . . . In front of us were two cars with two

or three Gestapo agents standing in front. . . . They said, "All those over eighteen on one side, and all the ones under eighteen on the other side." . . . What actually happened was that a train was coming from western Germany, going through different towns, picking up Polish Jews who were being sent . . . to the Polish border. . . . So the ones over eighteen were taken away, and we never saw them again.[13]

After the war started and Germany occupied huge chunks of Poland, the Nazis rounded up the Jews—men, women, and children—and crammed them into tiny sections of cities they

The site of the Wannsee Conference that coordinated and finalized a plan already in motion, the "final solution to the Jewish question."

THE CONCENTRATION CAMPS

called ghettos to await the "final solution." Sometime in October or November 1941, the Nazis decided what they would do. In the east, under cover of war, they would kill them.

The Nazis had already begun killing Jews in the Soviet Union. As the German armies invaded, mobile killing squads called *Einsatzgruppen* followed them, gathering Jews by the hundreds and thousands in Soviet cities and shooting them. But the killing squads could not easily murder the nine million Jews of Europe. The leaders of all the government agencies that dealt with Jewish affairs met to decide on a more efficient method. At a conference in Wannsee, a suburb of Berlin, on January 20, 1942, they agreed on exactly how they would implement the "final solution." They would deport all the Jews from the ghettos to forced labor camps. They would work them hard, feed them little, and expect them to die. Those who survived would be killed. They would build killing centers—death camps—for that purpose.

At the close of the Wannsee Conference, Heinrich Himmler, head of all the police forces of Germany, sent an order to the chief inspector of the concentration camps. He told him to prepare to receive, in one month, one hundred thousand Jewish men and fifty thousand Jewish women. Thus, by February 1942, the Nazi camps had become places for the abuse, torture, and murder of all of Europe's Jews.

YOUTH DESTROYED—THE NAZI CAMPS

The Nazis eventually established more than twenty thousand camps, including six death camps. This map shows the major concentration, transit, forced labor, and death camps.

Chapter Two

WAITING ROOMS

Heinrich Himmler's initial order was for the camps to "employ" 150,000 Jews. But his ultimate goal was for the system to dispose of 9 million. Even the more than twenty thousand camps that were eventually built could not handle that many people at once. In Poland and other parts of eastern Europe, the ghettos held the Jews until the Nazi camps had room for them. In the west, captured Jews waited in transit camps.

From Refuge to Detention

During the 1930s, as antisemitism fueled greater persecution in Germany, thousands of Jews fled. Many went to France, Belgium, Luxembourg, or the Netherlands, where Jewish communities already existed. But Hitler's armies followed them. On May 10, 1940, Germany invaded all four countries.

At that time, France had some refugee camps near its southern border with Spain. They had been put together quickly for the Spaniards fleeing from civil war in their country. As the German tanks moved west and south, the Jews in western Europe sped farther west, to the south of France. There, many found shelter in the refugee camps.

Nine-year-old Peter Feigl had lived in three countries before coming to France. Born in Berlin, Germany, he was in Austria

Peter Feigl and his family were taken to the Gurs concentration camp in France. These are pages from Peter's diary. The two photographs are of Peter's parents, who died during the war. The right page is dated "New Year 1943."

WAITING ROOMS

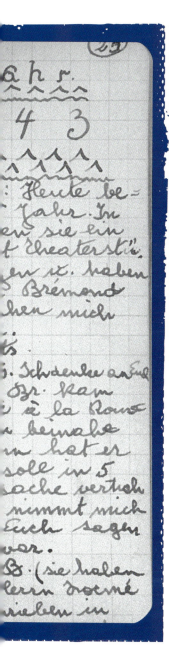

when Germany took over that country. His family escaped to Belgium, then to France:

[My mother] goes to the prefecture [government office] and . . . [after] about four or five times of being sent from one to the other, someone finally said to her, "Ah, Madame, we know exactly how to deal with cases such as yours. There is a place. It's called Oloron Ste. Marie. It's in the Pyrenees [mountains between France and Spain]. You go there and they know exactly how to deal with cases such as yours." So with the little money that my mother had left, she buys a railway ticket to Oloron Ste. Marie.[1]

When the Feigls reached Oloron Ste. Marie, they found that the camp was no longer a refugee camp:

As we arrive at the railway station, the train is surround[ed] with French gendarmes [police] with machine guns. And they take us off the train and put us on trucks, and the next stop was a French concentration camp called Camp De Gurs. . . . Gurs was a camp in the Pyrenees mountains which had been built in the 1930s by the French to house the

29

> fleeing Spanish . . . and suddenly this camp had been turned into a holding camp or a concentration camp.²

As war was looming, the French were afraid the foreigners in their country might side with an enemy if and when war started. They decided to intern anyone from a country that might become an enemy nation. Thus, they turned the refugee camps into detention facilities for foreigners. Many of those people were Jews who had escaped from Germany, Austria, and Czechoslovakia.

Interning More Jews

By June 1940, Germany occupied and controlled the northern part of France. France was allowed to keep control of the south, but only as a puppet of the Nazis. The capital of the unoccupied south was the city of Vichy, so southern France was known as Vichy France. The Vichy government continued to arrest and detain foreign Jews in a number of detention camps: Argeles, Saint-Cyprien, Le Vernet, Les Milles, Gurs, and the family camp of Rivesaltes.

None of the camps was pleasant. Sixteen-year-old Hanna Hirsch was appalled at the conditions:

> Gurs was a camp full of mud. It was clay. When it rained, you sank into the clay up to your knees. . . . One woman we lost really choked to death in the mud. She went at night to the latrine. She fell. She could not extricate herself and she died. So our experiences were horrendous. It is not . . . I would not say Gurs was Auschwitz, but it was what they called the little Hell before the big one, meaning Auschwitz.³

Because Rivesaltes was designated as a family camp, many people with children were sent there. But it was no better than the others. Having her family with her could not hide the horrors of the camp from ten-year-old Eva Lang:

> We were terribly hungry, and all around there were rows of barbed wire and guard towers a few meters away. Everything was grey, dismal and dirty. There was the constant noise of the wind blowing between the huts, the muddiness of the stony ground during the rainy days and then a torrid, dry heat because it was still summer. People coughed, wandered, died. The lack of water and its mediocre quality heightened

Eva Lang with her sister Rivka in St. Jean-de-Vedas, France, after their release from the Rivesaltes camp in 1941. Eva and her family suffered in the terrible conditions at Rivesaltes.

the appalling sanitary conditions, and this encouraged the spread of . . . epidemics such as dysentery.[4]

Although France controlled the camps in the south, the Vichy government cooperated with the Nazis. In 1940, the Nazis were still expelling Jews from Germany. They forced the French to take the German Jews into their camps. Max Liebmann was nineteen when he and his mother were deported from Germany to Gurs:

Well, the beginning of course, was very chaotic. . . . The first night, we didn't even have our luggage. The luggage was brought the next morning. It was just dumped in the rain and . . . was lying in a big pile and we had to find our luggage. . . . Every time it rained, people would fall in the mud, particularly the old people. The food was abominable. We had very little to eat.[5]

In occupied northern France, Jews began to be arrested in May 1941. In that month, 6,500 foreign Jews living in Paris, men ages eighteen to sixty, received ominous cards that read:

Mr. _____ is invited to present himself in person, accompanied by one member of his family or by one friend, at 7:00 in the morning on May 14, 1941, for an examination of his situation. He is asked to provide identification. Those who do not present themselves on the set day and hour are liable for the most severe sanctions.[6]

Some of the men went into hiding or tried to escape, but most obeyed the order. As Marcel Skurnik said, "I decided to present myself because the rumor was that those who did not go . . . would harm their families, who would be mistreated and seized in their place."[7]

Most, however, feared the worst. Céline Stene recalled later: "I followed him [my husband] and I saw that his face was bathed in tears. The children clung to him and would not separate from him, as if they had a presentiment [strong feeling] that they would never see him again."[8]

The men were taken to one of two camps in the north: Pithiviers or Beaune-la-Rolande.

> "I followed him [my husband] and I saw that his face was bathed in tears."

From Detention to Transit

The pace of arrests picked up in 1942, just after the Wannsee Conference. Once the Nazis decided that the solution to the "Jewish problem" was wholesale murder, children as well as men and women were brought to the camps. At that point, the detention centers became transit camps—places where Jews would wait until transportation could be arranged "to the east," to the killing centers. Several transit camps were located in western Europe: Drancy and Compiégne in France, Mechelen in Belgium, Fünfbrunnen in Luxembourg, and Vught and Westerbork in the Netherlands.

The largest transit camp in France was Drancy. Ernest Koenig, twenty-three when Germany invaded France, spent two years in the Le Vernet detention camp before being transferred to Drancy:

Drancy was the largest transit camp in France. Armand Rubinsztejn sent this postcard to his family interned at Drancy in 1943.

> After perhaps twenty-four hours [on a train] we came to Drancy. . . . Drancy consisted of barracks . . . which had been made for the French police before the war and which could not be occupied because they were wet and badly built, so they stood empty . . . before Drancy became a concentration camp. . . . It was full of . . . barbed wire. . . . We were put into rooms which were full of rotten straw. . . . We didn't know what's going to happen to us but we knew, of course, we are now in the clutches of the Germans. And at night we heard sometimes shooting from other parts of the camp. We didn't know what it means. I remember I went to one of the barbed wires and . . . tried to see whether I can get out, but it was out of the question.[9]

Leo Bretholz also thought about escape. At nineteen, he had been interned in St. Cyprian as a foreign Jew, and he had climbed the camp's fence to freedom. A year later, he was arrested again and sent to Rivesaltes. From there he was transferred to Drancy:

> By that time, we in the south had heard of Drancy but did not quite realize the immensity of the camp and the tragedy involved in that preparation towards deportation. . . . In that train [going to Drancy], several times going to the washroom, I looked the situation over. Escape was always on my mind. . . . But there was no getting away from that bathroom because the gendarmes stood right in front of the door when somebody went to

> the bathroom. They were in the car with us. It was not like the gendarmes were riding in another car ahead, or in the back so that they should be there in case of emergency. They were with us in the train. . . . Each compartment had their own door to walk in, so was no use trying it.[10]

When he arrived at Drancy, Bretholz found the transit camp in the occupied north much worse than the detention camps of the south:

> Drancy was a complex that was built to be a military barracks facility. It was a multi-story complex almost like a stadium because it was round. But due to the war, beginning of the war, that structure was never finished. So the places, the rooms that they put us in were wide open, concrete floor with piping laying around and half-installed electrical wires, half-installed plumbing, makeshift, and it was concrete. Windows—no windows. There were no panes in the windows. It was just the opening where the windows were supposed to go in the frames later. That wasn't done so it was all open, breezy. And on this concrete: straw. Men, women, children together. Minimal facilities to wash. . . . One trough where . . . the water ran down in a trickle. Minimum toilet facilities. Watchtowers. Barbed wire. Suburb of Paris close to "civilization." Minimal food distribution.[11]

Leo Bretholz lived through the dehumanization process at Drancy. When he was on a transport to Auschwitz, Bretholz jumped off the train but ended up in a French prison. While in solitary confinement, Bretholz made many drawings, writings, and puzzles, including this drawing from February 6, 1943.

From the moment he arrived, Bretholz could see in the actions of the camp police and the eyes of those already living in the camp that "it was not [the detention camp of] Rivesaltes by any stretch of the imagination":

> The checking-in process in Drancy was, well, a first step in a real dehumanization process. . . . We went through a barrack process of checking in which would also mean taking your watch away, your rings, certain belongings, money. And another psychological ploy: giving you a receipt for the things that they took from you, with the admonition, "Don't lose that!" [It was a pretense] because you will never get them back. "That is your receipt that has a number on it." It had a number on it. Just imagine that! And people there tried to sort of whisper to us that this isn't good here.[12]

The pretense of fairness, of some sort of normalcy, was even stronger in other transit camps. William Lowenberg, sixteen when he and his family were interned in Westerbork in 1942, remembered the transit camp as "civilized" compared to what he would endure later:

> There was a whole community of life. . . . Children would go to school. They had a wonderful orchestra. Then they had opera and theater. Because there was a whole element of German Jews who had come from Berlin mostly, from the stages, intellectual community, the artists developed in Westerbork an infrastructure of some very

WAITING ROOMS

A group portrait of Jewish school children and their teachers at the Westerbork transit camp on June 8, 1942. The Nazis used schools, music, and the arts as a way to hide the fact that the transit camps were simply waiting rooms for the death camps.

> beautiful entertainment. For me it was beautiful because I came from a small town and I had never been to opera before in my life. . . . In Westerbork you could read. In the camp there were some books. . . . I don't know if there was a movie there, I don't remember that, but it was—I know we were talking about the entertainment they had there. They had a large auditorium. I remember that. And evenings there were . . . lectures there.[13]

School, music, and theater—like the receipts for items that would never be returned—were charades. They were acts masking the fact that the transit camps were merely the waiting rooms for the death camps. Irene Hasenberg was only thirteen when she was sent to Westerbork, but she sensed the truth:

> Most people didn't stay very long in Westerbork, and that depended on . . . what kind of category you were in. There were all kinds of lists and all kinds of categories depending on who you were and what kind of privileges you bought yourself. . . . The Jews paid thousands and thousands of guilders to get on a list and were promised they would not be deported. They could stay in Westerbork, and of course eventually everyone was deported, practically everyone.

"They could stay in Westerbork, and of course eventually everyone was deported, practically everyone."

> So you bought time. If you had money, you could buy time. If you had some other characteristic that allowed you to be in a group that was not deported yet, then you could buy time.[14]

But in 1943, when Hasenberg entered Westerbork, time was running out for all the Jews. Those in the transit camps knew that deportation was their eventual fate. In Drancy, Leo Bretholz knew that deportation meant something awful, but he did not know exactly what:

> We saw utter despair, uncertainty, acts of aggression, pushing, shoving, end of rifle butts, and threats. And it wasn't until I saw a newborn baby being shot like a clay pigeon, and the mother being killed too because she threw herself into the path of the bullet, that I . . . said, " . . . If this can happen in Drancy, what can we expect where we're going to? This is France. This is not yet Germany."[15]

As bad as the transit camp was, Bretholz could not imagine the horror that awaited him in the next camp.

Chapter Three

WORKED TO DEATH

As the war continued, and especially after the Wannsee Conference, the number and size of labor camps grew. Already established camps were expanded and new camps were built. The Nazis used the camp inmates to build the new facilities. Siegfried Halbreich helped build Gross-Rosen, a satellite camp of Sachsenhausen in Germany (now Poland)—a subcamp that grew so large it became an independent camp with ninety-seven subcamps:

> The conditions were there much worse than in Sachsenhausen. During the day, we had to march to the stone quarry, I would say maybe 20 minutes away, and it was in a mountainous terrain. . . . We had to work in this quarry carrying the heavy rocks, and people died like flies. On the way back, we had to everyone carry one big rock on our shoulders to the camp.
> . . . And we had to continue to build the camp till twelve o'clock at night . . . all without food. When we came to the barracks, we were so tired that we just didn't have any appetite. We fall asleep. And in the morning, five, six o'clock right away, up and again the same thing.[1]

To get their prisoners from the transit camps to the labor camps, the Nazis used deception. Irene Hasenberg, fourteen when she was transported to forced labor in Bergen-Belsen, had been told that her new home would be far nicer than the lice- and rat-infested quarters of Westerbork:

> We were in a passenger train this time, not the cattle cars that we had been shipped in going to Westerbork. And we all thought that we were going to a better camp. . . . From now on things were going to be better—we would be in an inter-nation camp, we would have more food, we would be treated in a civil manner.[2]

But from the moment Hasenberg reached the camp in Germany, she knew the Nazi promises were lies:

> We were met by SS with big German shepherds. . . . That was a custom of the Nazis, they had dogs. Dogs that they would . . . use to threaten and sometimes use in reality. And, we had to walk quite a distance. And they were keeping everybody in line, hundreds of people marching along. . . . It was very dreary. It was larger, the barracks were very different. People were stuffed into barracks, many more people into smaller space. All of that became apparent right away. And because the Jews administered Westerbork, and this was not the case in Bergen-Belsen, the treatment was a totally different way of being treated from the very beginning. And . . . it was apparent right away that things were not better here. This was not a better place than Westerbork.[3]

YOUTH DESTROYED—THE NAZI CAMPS

Gross-Rosen began as a satellite camp, but grew so large it eventually became an independent camp. This five-sided badge issued to Helen Waterford identified her as a prisoner from the Kratzau-Chrastava labor camp, a satellite camp of Gross-Rosen.

In fact, all the forced labor camps were places of indescribable filth, stench, disease, hunger, humiliation, torture, and death. Samuel, Bernard, and Nathan Offen—brothers in their teens and early twenties—were deported from the ghetto of Krakow, Poland, to the camp of Płaszow. Samuel described the transition: "A horrible life started. . . . There were thousands of us concentrated in a small camp behind electrified barbed wires. And guards and machine gun towers, search lights at night, dogs. . . . We had it terrible. SS-Nazi, SS guards. They were just shooting people at will."[4]

Kinds of Work

The purpose of these camps was two-fold. They were to furnish labor for Germany, particularly for the war effort. And they were to provide means whereby many Jews would die "naturally." The prisoners were put to work at all kinds of back-breaking jobs. At fifteen, Marton Adler helped build the housing at Dora, a subcamp of Dachau:

> ```
> [We] built barracks, prefabricated barracks.
> A section of a barrack even today you
> really need four strong guys to carry
> those. Very, very heavy. So they put four
> guys to [carry a] section to . . . [the]
> top of a hill. I couldn't, honest to God, I
> couldn't even if they put the thing on me.
> I'd collapse. But all the three were grown
> ups so the other three carried it and I was
> supposed to be the fourth one. I can't even
> reach it with my hand. . . . The other
> three had to carry my load.[5]
> ```

In addition to construction, some prisoners were kept busy at rebuilding. A factory at the Magdeburg camp was frequently hit by bombs from Allied planes. Fifteen-year-old Paul Molnar helped repair the damage:

> ```
> We cleared debris, we unloaded lumber, we
> unloaded cement, we unloaded metal things.
> Whatever they told us, unloaded brick,
> we just worked there and did all sorts of
> jobs. And then at twelve we got fifteen
> minutes off and we got fed again and then
> we went back to work. And we worked 'til
> six o'clock. At six o'clock we were marched
> ```

YOUTH DESTROYED—THE NAZI CAMPS

Prisoners working near railroad tracks at the entrance to the Buchenwald concentration camp in Germany. The Nazis forced the camp prisoners to assist in the war effort.

back to the camp. And if anybody died or was beaten to death or if anything happened to them . . . we had to carry them back to the camp. Nobody could stay behind because when we got back we had to line up again at the square or Platz and everybody was counted, everybody had to be accounted for there—as many left came back. And sometimes it took a long time. . . . After it was done . . . we got fed again. And we collapsed, we went to sleep, we got up [at] four o'clock, we did the same routine, seven days a week.[6]

Labor camp inmates built roads in Germany. Sam Seltzer, fourteen when the war began, was sent from Poland to the Klettendorf and Geppersdorf camps in Germany:

> We built the Autobahn. I was put in with . . . my brother's . . . friend. . . . We were paired up to load up sand . . . into the cars and then they took [it] over to the place where they need sand for the Autobahn. They dumped it out and they brought it back. And we had to lay the tracks. . . . You had to cut black dirt away . . . and just load the sand. . . . That was my first . . . hard work.[7]

The work was especially hard for young people not used to heavy labor. David Bergman was doing a man's job at thirteen years of age:

> In Reichenbach [subcamp of Gross-Rosen, the Nazi said], "We need bricklayers." Now, since I was a professional bricklayer (laughing), I right away raised my hand. And I was put into a work group. It was very, very, very difficult work. We had to march several miles to work. I was already half dead when I already got to work. Then to work yet, it took all the strength just to make it through the marching. Then, when we marched back, if a person was not physically able to complete the march, they just shot him on the spot.[8]

The most important work of the camps was the production of weapons and related products. David Kahan was fifteen when he helped build an airplane factory near the Müldorf camp. To protect it from Allied air strikes, it was built underground:

> It was all woods. They have given us handsaws and . . . we sawed the huge trees off. . . . After the area was cleared, we started to dig ditches . . . [with] shovels and picks. . . . We dug this huge underground bunker. It was supposed to be strong enough that no bombs that was known in those days could penetrate it. The concrete must have been at least two feet thick, or maybe thicker.[9]

Women and girls were not exempt from the brutal labor of the work camps. Hannah Fisk worked ten- and twelve-hour days in Gabersdorf, a women's camp:

> I went to [a cotton] factory. . . . They made fabrics. . . . [The cotton] was very heavy—I was fifteen years old. I was carrying between 200 and 300 pounds [of] cotton. . . . When they [are] dry, they are nothing, but when they [are] wet, they [are] very heavy. I used to go like that. I was fifteen years old. But somehow I survived.[10]

Madeline Deutsch worked in an ammunition factory at Peterswaldan, a subcamp of Gross-Rosen. Near the end of the war, as the Soviet armies marched toward the camp, fifteen-year-old Madeline had to do heavy work alongside the men:

> They utilized us for digging fox holes because the front was getting closer and closer. . . . I must have weighed maybe,

if I was lucky, fifty, sixty pounds. I was like a skeleton. I was very small to start with. When I had to pick up this shovel in order to dig these ditches, it was heavier than I was. . . . But I had to keep digging and I had to try because . . . those who didn't were . . . shot. . . . How I lasted, I'll never know.[11]

Some work was easier than others. Occasionally, the guards singled out the younger inmates to be their personal servants. Sometimes they would place children in the better positions. Marton Adler eventually received such an assignment at Dora:

Women were not exempt from the brutal forced labor of the Nazi camps. These Soviet female workers stand outside a factory in a labor camp in Germany on April 27, 1942.

> Somehow or other, I was picked by the SS man . . . to work in that clothing depot . . . sorting clothes. . . . I had sort of a privileged position. I had one of the best jobs you could get. I was envied by everybody. . . . Dora was already a bad camp, very, very, terrible camp. . . . That really saved me, that job. . . . Once I worked in that, I wasn't exposed to the elements, I had a roof over my head, I wasn't beaten. . . . Sorting clothes is not digging ditches in the rain and going to sleep in the soaked clothes.[12]

"Sorting clothes is not digging ditches in the rain and going to sleep in the soaked clothes."

Occasionally, the Nazis found a use for the children who were too young and weak to do hard manual labor. Abraham Malach was only nine when he was taken to Starachowice: "I was not with the work squads that were going outside the camp working in factories, whether it was munitions or whatever for the Germans. So I cleaned the police barracks and I served as a messenger boy."[13]

Death in the Labor Camps

The labor camps were designed for both work and death. The difficulty of the work and the lack of food and rest made for a lethal combination. Fifteen-year-old David Kahan watched older, stronger men die while building a bridge outside Müldorf:

> The hardest work was to walk up with those 100-pound cement bags about—there were

> approximately thirty steps where the cement mixer was mixing water with the powder. And to carry those bags on your shoulder was just, it was devastating. We didn't get enough food, and . . . I saw most of the people collapsing from carrying those cement bags up to the mixer.[14]

Any who collapsed but were still breathing did not last long. They were often killed on the spot or taken to a camp that had gas chambers that killed more efficiently. Kahan saw many of his fellow inmates taken out of Müldorf:

> People who just picked 'em up and dragged 'em away. And if . . . it was a temporary collapse that they could recuperate, they came back to work. If they were too weak, they were taken back to the Mühldorf camp and they had sort of a hospital-like place where they kept 'em. . . . People died from hard labor, but there was no gas chamber in Mühldorf, no extermination. So they used to keep . . . those who were weak . . . and then they loaded 'em in cattle cars and I think they took 'em to Dachau. . . . Dachau wasn't very far from us. That's where they were actually gassed, in Dachau. . . . When you were too weak . . . they had no use for you of course. They only had use for you if you could work.[15]

Death also came at the hands of guards who were not satisfied with the inmates' work. Harry Prow was frightened because he did not know how to do the job he was given in the underground factory at Dora:

YOUTH DESTROYED—THE NAZI CAMPS

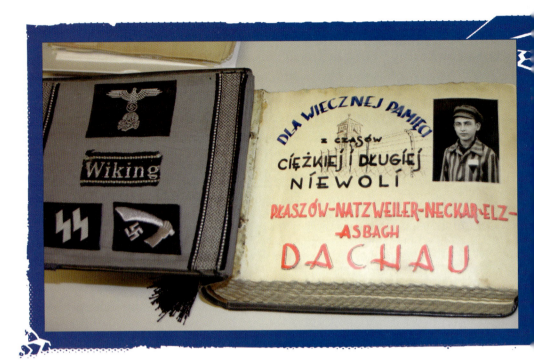

These pages are from an album of ink-and-watercolor drawings that convey the brutality of Dachau. Arnold Unger, a Holocaust survivor who committed suicide in 1972, brought the album to America as an orphan. The artist of the album is believed to be Michal Porluski.

They assigned me to a metal bench, something I have never seen in my life. I was twenty-two years old. I had never seen a machine shop, period, let alone a metal bench. I didn't even know what it was. And they told me to stay and look what the guy [next to me] was doing. . . . The guy at the machine was a Russian . . . prisoner. Well, the next day I came back to the next night shift, the Russian guy was gone. You couldn't ask no questions where he is or what happened. They just told me, "This is what you have to do." There was a guy

> with a machine gun . . . behind everybody's
> back there. There was always a guy—you
> didn't know what to do but you couldn't
> ask for what you're supposed to do. . . .
> You couldn't even turn around [to] look at
> the guy because he just as soon shoot you.
> If you told him you didn't know, you were
> gone. Either you do or you die.[16]

The camp guards made sure the unproductive people served as examples to the rest. Prow recalled: "They always had gallows there. One morning we had—it must have been about twenty or thirty people that they hung during the night. And that was a daily routine, day in and day out."[17]

Kahan, even at his young age, knew that how well he performed at his job in Müldorf meant the difference between life and death:

> I was part of the cement crew . . . because
> of my youth. There weren't very many people
> at my age who were picked to be alive.
> . . . I would say that was a miracle.
> . . . I wasn't tall and, you know, many,
> many boys at my age were sent to the gas
> chamber. There was a small minority of
> fifteen-year-olds. I believe that I am one of
> the youngest survivors in this town. There's
> a few maybe who are younger than I am, but
> fifteen was a lucky number. Most of 'em
> were seventeen, eighteen, nineteen, twenty,
> more developed, stronger people. . . . You
> had to be brave and practically took your
> life in your hands. Because if they caught
> you willfully, you know, not working, you
> know, they probably beat, beat, beat you

half to death or they reported you to the SS and took you back to the camp and that was it. You know, you were done.[18]

In the I. B. Farben factory at Magdeburg, fifteen-year-old Paul Molnar learned that brutal work, sadistic beatings, and indiscriminate shooting were not the only means of torture and death:

> They let one of their dogs, the German dogs, loose on me, and he chewed up my right calf. . . . I couldn't get up, I couldn't move. So a lot of times when they did things like that, when they were all done with you, they just take a revolver and shoot you. But in my case, for whatever reason, they thought it was really hilarious and they started laughing and they walked away from me and I laid there on the ground. . . . I knew that you had to make it back to the camp, because if you don't make it back to the camp, you will be shot and carried back. Well, there was no way that I could walk. There was no way. I couldn't stand up because my right leg . . . was totally useless to me. . . . My cousin and another boy . . . grabbed me and we got into the middle of the pack and I put my arms around their shoulders and I could hobble on my left leg and they literally carried me four miles.[19]

One of the most brutal forced labor camps was Mauthausen. In early 1941, it was reclassified as the only category III camp—with the harshest of conditions for the most serious offenders. Franz Zieres, commander of the camp, was shot trying to escape when the camp was liberated. On his deathbed, he described how inmates were treated:

> Himmler gave the order to load a 45-kilo [99-pound] stone on an inmate's back and make him run around with it until he fell dead. . . . The inmates had to haul stones until they collapsed, then they were shot and their record was annotated "Trying to escape." Others were driven into a fence made of charged high-tension wire. Others were literally torn to pieces by the dog named "Lord" belonging to the camp commander Bachmeyer, who sicced it on the inmates. Inmates of the camp office were ordered to assemble in the court yard [and] they were shot like wild animals. . . . SS men were trained on the rifle ranges where inmates were used as targets.[20]

"Inmates of the camp office were ordered to assemble in the court yard [and] they were shot like wild animals."

Fred Ferber was fourteen, too young for such strenuous work. He was one of the privileged children at Mauthausen. But he still lived in fear:

> I was younger than most. . . . I was on the inside kommando [work detail] most of the time, cleaning the barracks. Extremely lucky. . . . They give you a stone on your . . . shoulder. And you have to go to a hundred and twenty-five, hundred and

YOUTH DESTROYED—THE NAZI CAMPS

Prisoners carry heavy stones up the "stairs of death" from a quarry at the Mauthausen labor camp. Mauthausen was one of the most brutal forced labor camps.

forty steps. I don't remember at the moment how many. [There were actually 186 steps.] . . . And anyone who couldn't make it got beat up—hit. And if you really couldn't make it, when you got up . . . they push you down [into] the quarry. . . . The life was over. . . . So it was terrible fear of not carrying the stone up. Everybody was working in fear. Every day a number of people were killed.[21]

Young Children

What of the younger children in the labor camps—the ones too small to clean barracks, polish the guards' shoes, or act as messengers? The ones of no economic use to the Nazis? Sometimes children were allowed to stay with their parents in some camps. But they could not interfere with the work of the inmates. Noemi Engel had vivid memories of a camp near Vienna, Austria, even though she was only three when she was interned:

> I was left in the barrack all day long when my mother went to work. And my mother worked a shift and a half so she would get more food to give to my brother and I. And I asked her . . . "Where was I? What did you do with me?" . . . And so she told me that there was an old lady, . . . a grandmother, who was there with her family and she was in our barrack and she would watch me. Anyway one time apparently one of the guards came in. And I know there was snow on the ground. And he kicked me out in the snow. I was in my underwear. It was scary. I was very scared.[22]

The labor camps were obviously frightening places for small children. All too often, their parents were not able to protect them from the cruelty of the Nazis. They had to figure out how to cope on their own. An eight-year-old named Martin adjusted to the atrocities at Skarzysko-Kemienna by becoming hard and mean to other people:

> You saw beating and shooting. . . . My father, my brother, and I were taken in one direction. My mother was immediately put into another camp. . . . I saw children just falling by the wayside. People dying. . . . I trained myself to be very brutal, very cold. And . . . sometimes I think I was made too inhuman. Because I didn't care about anybody else.[23]

The ruthlessness of life in the camps made caring about others more difficult. Bernard Klein, fifteen years old when interned in Gliewitz, was shocked to see a young boy with little regard for his ailing father:

> People were dehumanized by all this. When his son came to see his father [in the camp infirmary] the next morning, and he was told his father is dead, the first question was "Where is his bread ration?" . . . And the second was to reach in his father's mouth to see if he can pull out the gold tooth so he can sell it for another slice of bread.[24]

As heartless and bestial as the forced labor camps were, they were not the worst part of the Holocaust. On December 8, 1941, the Nazis opened the first of six death camps.

Chapter Four

THE DEATH CAMPS

Hitler was not squeamish about having people killed. Soon after becoming chancellor of Germany, he ordered the executions of scores of men he considered threats to his rule. He began a world war knowing it would lead to thousands of deaths. But killing children—would anyone deliberately take the lives of innocent children? Yes, Hitler did.

Hitler wanted to create a "master race" of German people without any flaws. He had no problem simply eliminating anyone he thought was "unfit." In October 1939, he issued orders for euthanasia, or "mercy killing," of patients in mental institutions and people with physical defects. He ordered doctors to kill hospital patients who were not likely to recover. The stated purpose was to relieve people of their suffering. The actual goal was to relieve the government of the expense of their care and to rid society of any "defects." This program was known by its code name, T4.

Euthanasia Institutes

Many of the victims of the T4 mercy killings were children. Robert Wagemann was only five when his parents were told he needed a physical exam. Because of an injury to his hip at birth, Wagemann had a disability:

> During the examination my mom was sitting on the outside of the room, and she

> overheard a conversation that the doctors would do away with me, would "abspritz" me, which means that they would give me a needle and put me to sleep. My mom overheard the conversation and during lunch time, while the doctors were gone, she grabbed hold of me. We went down to the Neckar River into the high reeds and . . . went into hiding because now we knew that they really were after us.[1]

In the T4 program, five centers, called euthanasia institutes, were set up in Germany and one in southern Austria. At first, patients were killed by lethal injection—poison shot directly into their veins. But very quickly, Nazi ingenuity found a much more efficient way of killing. Viktor Brack, who was hanged for his part in the "mercy killings" after the war, explained at his trial:

> A room suitable in the hospital was used, a room of necessity attached to the reception ward and to the room where the insane persons were kept. This room was made into a gas chamber. It was sealed, given special doors and windows, and then a few meters of gas piping were laid, or some kind of piping with holes in it. Outside this room there was a container, a compressed gas container with the necessary apparatus.[2]

The euthanasia institutes also had to have a way to dispose of the bodies of those who were murdered there. Brack testified:

> When the room had been cleared of gas again, stretchers were brought in and the bodies were carried into an adjoining room.

THE DEATH CAMPS

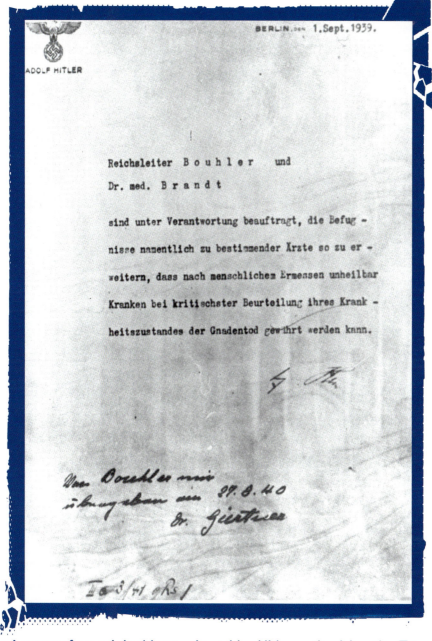

A copy of an original letter signed by Hitler authorizing the T4 program. In the letter, Hitler states that persons "suffering from illnesses judged to be incurable may . . . be granted a mercy death." The Nazis used this program to murder people they did not believe fit into their "master race."

> There the doctor examined them to determine whether they were dead. . . . When the doctor had determined death, he freed the bodies for cremation and then they were cremated. . . . Crematoriums were built in the institutions.[3]

The doctors appeared to convince themselves that killing people who were not perfectly "fit," mentally or physically, was a kindness to the patients and a duty to their country. Brack thought the entire operation was quite humane:

> [The] requirement was that the killing should not only be painless, but also imperceptible [that is, the patient should not realize he or she is about to be killed]. For this reason, the photographing of the patients, which was only done for scientific reasons, took place before they entered the chambers, and the patients were completely diverted [or distracted] thereby. Then they were led into the gas chamber, which they were told was a shower room. . . . I was . . . convinced that the method was painless. And I also saw that by this method the patient did not realize that he was about to be killed. There were benches and chairs in the chamber. A few minutes after the gas was let in, the patient became sleepy and tired and died after a few minutes. They simply went to sleep without even knowing that they were going to sleep, and that was one of the most essential requirements.[4]

Himmler recognized that the T4 method of execution was far more efficient than the rifles used on "difficult" inmates of the concentration camps. After the euthanasia institutes were established, prisoners from the labor camps were transported to the centers for "special treatment," a code term for mass murder. But once the "final solution" was put into motion, six euthanasia centers were not enough. Each could kill only twenty to thirty people at a time in a small room. Besides, all six were in Germany or Austria, where prying minds might eventually object.

> "A few minutes after the gas was let in, the patient became sleepy and tired and died after a few minutes."

"Operation Reinhard"

The Nazis decided to build camps devoted entirely to killing Jews. They began construction on the first camp, Chelmno, in late 1941. After Reinhard Heydrich, Himmler's second in command, was assassinated in May 1942, they named the scheme to solve the "Jewish Problem" with special death camps "Operation Reinhard." The plan was that the Jews from the ghettos would be brought to the camps and killed as soon as they arrived. The process would be repeated until the ghettos were completely empty and all the Jews were dead.

Between March and July 1942, three Operation Reinhard camps were added to the camp system: Belzec, Sobibor, and Treblinka. Two other camps—Majdanek and Auschwitz—were refitted as annihilation camps. All six death camps were in Poland.

They were near railroad lines so Jews could be brought easily and in large numbers. And they were far enough from populated areas that their grim business would remain somewhat secret.

Chelmno

The first death camp was outside the remote town of Chelmno, built to kill Jews from the ghetto of Lodz, Poland. It began operating on December 8, 1941, in a large mansion the Nazis called "the castle." A ramp was installed that led not to a gas chamber, but to one of five gas vans. One of the men who drove a gas van, Walter Burmeister, explained how the process worked:

> As soon as the ramp had been erected in the castle, people started arriving. . . . The people were told that they had to take a bath, that their clothes had to be disinfected and that they could hand in any valuable items beforehand to be registered. . . .
> When they had undressed, they were sent to the cellar of the castle, and then along a passageway on to the ramp, and from there into the gas van. In the castle there were signs marked "to the baths." The gas vans were large vans. . . . The interior walls were lined with sheet metal. On the floor there was a wooden grille. The floor of the van had an opening which could be connected to the exhaust by means of a removable metal pipe. When the lorries [vans] were full of people, the double doors at the back were closed and the exhaust connected to the interior of the van. . . .
> The Kommando member detailed as driver would start the engine right away so that

THE DEATH CAMPS

A large group of men seated on the ground in the Chelmno death camp. Aside from a few people to be chosen to work in the *Sonderkommando*, all prisoners were killed upon arrival.

```
the people inside the lorry were suffocated
by the exhaust gases. Once this had taken
place, the union between the exhaust and
the inside of the lorry was disconnected
and the van was driven to the camp in the
woods, where the bodies were unloaded. In
the early days, they were initially burned
in mass graves, later incinerated. . . . I
then drove the van back to the castle and
parked it there. Here it would be cleaned
of the excretions of the people that had
died in it. Afterwards it would once again
be used for gassing.⁵
```

From each transport brought to the camp, a few would be pulled aside to work in the *Sonderkommando*. This was the special squad that cleaned up after the killings. They generally worked for a few days, then they were shot and a new group took their places. Simon Srebnik, only thirteen, was selected from his group. One of the Nazis took a liking to him, and he remained at his assignment for several months. He miraculously survived the executioner's bullet and lived to describe the work of the Sonderkommando at Chelmno:

> When the gas vans would arrive, the SS would say, "Open the doors!" And we would open the doors, and the corpses would fall out. And . . . two men would get in . . . and one would grab the feet and the other the [head and pull the bodies out]. . . . The people who had gold teeth in their mouth—[a man] would go up to them with his pliers and pull the teeth. . . . And there were SS who would shout, "Throw them in [to the ovens] quicker, throw them in quicker. Look, another truck is arriving!" And it was like that all day long.[6]

"The people who had gold teeth in their mouth—[a man] would go up to them with his pliers and pull the teeth."

Seventeen-year-old Jakub Lapides lived in an orphanage in the Lodz ghetto with his brother and sister. Jakub witnessed the *Gehsperre Aktion*, a roundup of children and elderly Jews for deportation to Chelmno:

> One day they announced in our orphanage that we will travel to a different place, and we were told, "Take everything you can." We went out to wait for the trucks to take us. And then my brother Moshe said to me and Miriam, my sister: "Let's hide in the cemetery." We went and hid there among the gravestones. We saw people bringing huge pots with soup. We were very hungry and Moshe started to go back and we followed him to the food line. We hadn't gotten the soup yet, and the trucks arrived and I said, "Let's go back to the cemetery." I ran back. But not Moshe, and not Miriam; they did not come back. They were taken on the trucks.[7]

Jakub's brother and sister were among the 152,000 Jews killed at Chelmno.[8]

Belzec

The vans of Chelmno could kill a hundred to a hundred fifty people at a time. When the second death camp was built, it incorporated an "improved" method of killing: stationary gas chambers. German SS officer Kurt Gerstein was shocked when he saw what went on at Belzec, and he tried to stop it. He sent notes to leaders of other countries, but no one listened. After the war, he told everyone what he had witnessed:

> A [terrible] odor hung over the whole area. . . . There was a "dressing hut" with window for "valuables." Further on, a room with a hundred chairs—the Barber room. Then a corridor 150 meters long in the open air,

barbed wire on both sides, with signs: "To the baths and inhalants." In front of us, a building like a bath house; to the left and right, large concrete pots of geraniums or other flowers. On the roof, the Star of David.

The following morning, a little before seven there was announcement: "The first train will arrive in ten minutes!" A few minutes later a train arrived: . . . 45 cars with more than 6,000 people. Two hundred Ukrainians assigned to this work flung open the doors and drove the Jews out of the cars with leather whips. A loud speaker gave instructions: "Strip, even artificial limbs and glasses. Hand all money and valuables in at the 'valuables window.' Women and young girls are to have their hair cut in the 'barbers hut.'"

Then the march began. Barbed wire on both sides, in the rear two dozen Ukrainians with rifles. They drew near. . . . [I was] in front of the death chambers. Stark naked men, women, children, and cripples passed by. A tall SS man in the corner called to the unfortunates in a loud minister's voice: "Nothing is going to hurt you! Just breathe deep and it will strengthen your lungs. It's a way to prevent contagious diseases. It's a good disinfectant!" They asked him what was going to happen and he answered: "The men will have to work, build houses and streets. The women won't have to do that. They will be busy with the housework and the kitchen." This was the last hope for some of these poor people, enough

THE DEATH CAMPS

A group of Jewish forced laborers at Belzec. The camp was closed down at the end of 1940 and was rebuilt as a death camp in November 1941.

to make them march toward the death chambers without resistance. The majority knew everything; the smell betrayed it! They climbed the little wooden stairs and entered the gas chambers, most of them silently, pushed by those behind them. A Jewess of about forty with eyes like fire cursed the murderers; she disappeared into the gas chamber after being struck several times by Captain Wirth's [the camp's commander's] whip. Many prayed . . . SS men pushed the men into the chambers. "Fill it up," Wirth ordered; 700–800 people in 93 square meters. The door closed.[9]

When the door closed, a camp official started a diesel engine that pumped gas into the chambers. The engines did not always work properly. The day of Kurt Gerstein's visit, the equipment broke down:

> [The SS officer] tried to start the motor. It wouldn't start! . . . My stopwatch clocked it all: 50 minutes, 70 minutes, and the diesel still would not start. The men were waiting in the gas chambers. You could hear them weeping. . . . The diesel started after two hours and 49 minutes by my stopwatch. Twenty minutes later passed. You could see through the window that many were already dead after thirty minutes![10]

The most grisly part of the operation was left to the prisoners who had been allowed to live, at least for a few days. Gerstein explained:

> Jewish workers on the other side opened the wooden doors. They had been promised their lives in return for doing this horrible job, plus a small percentage of the money and valuables collected. The men were still standing, like columns of stones, with no room to fall or to lean. Even in the death you could tell the families, all holding hands. It was difficult to separate them while emptying the rooms for the next batch. The bodies were tossed out, bluer, wet with sweat and urine, the legs smeared with excrement. . . . Two dozen workers were busy checking mouths which they opened with iron hooks. "Gold to the left, no

```
gold to the right." Others checked [body
cavities], looking for money, diamonds,
gold, etc. Dentists knocked out gold teeth,
bridges, and crowns, with hammers.¹¹
```

When very young children were brought to Belzec, the Nazis sometimes did not use the gas chambers. Chaim Hirszman, a Jewish worker who tended the bodies of the dead and one of the few survivors of the camp, recalled a different method: "A transport of children up to three years of age arrived. The workers were told to dig a big hole into which the children were thrown and buried alive. I cannot forget how the earth rose, until the children suffocated."[12]

> "I cannot forget how the earth rose, until the children suffocated."

Belzec was constructed to dispose of Jews of the Lublin and Lvov ghettos. In eight months of operation, at least 434,500 were killed at Belzec.[13] It served as a model for another Operation Reinhard camp: Sobibor.

Sobibor

Sobibor was located in a remote area amid thick woods. It was surrounded by barbed-wire fences laced with tree branches. Should any would-be escapees make it past the fences, they would have to cross a deep trench filled with water and a series of land mines. Sobibor consisted of three camps, called *lagers*. Lager I housed the prisoners who were kept alive only to help operate the camp. Some worked in Lager II, where they prepared their fellow Jews for Lager III, where they were killed. Thomas Blatt described how they met their end: "The victims' final steps were taken on a

Victims were transported to Sobibor, like the other death camps, on railroad cattle cars. This is a railroad signal with an oil lamp that was used at the Sobibor train station.

sandy pathway . . . cynically called 'Himmelfahrtstrasse' (Heavenly Way). . . . The entrance . . . descended immediately into the gas chambers decorated with flowers and a Star of David."[14]

The Nazis often chose teens to live a little longer than the rest. Blatt was one of the Jewish prisoners permitted to stay alive to sort the clothing of the dead:

```
[The camp commandant]
ask[ed] the men,
"Who's a carpenter?
Who's a mechanic?"
And I was no
mechanic. What could
a fifteen-year-old
boy be? But I did
want to live so much. And wherever the Nazi
moved, my eyes went after him. . . . When
he was moving back and forth and our eyes
met . . . he stopped, looked at me, and
said, "Come out you, du kleine [little
one]." . . . My father didn't want [me] to
go out. He [the German] beat him. And later
when he assembled about forty people, he
told the rest to go in the same way [as] the
women [to the gas chamber], and he left. In
this way I started to work in Sobibor.
```
[15]

Those selected for work did not know at first what would happen to the others. Ada Lichtmann, a young teacher chosen to toil in the camp laundry, did not realize how fortunate she was:

> We heard word for word how [the SS officer] Michel, standing on a small table, convincingly calmed the people; he promised them that after the bath they would get back all their possessions, and said that the time had come for Jews to become productive members of society. They would presently all be sent to the Ukraine where they would be able to live and work. The speech inspired confidence and enthusiasm among the people. They applauded spontaneously and occasionally they even danced and sang.[16]

Treblinka

The same lies and deceptions were used at the third Operation Reinhard camp. Built near an existing labor camp, it was called Treblinka II. Its purpose was to murder the Jews of Warsaw, the largest of the ghettos. The unloading platform was made to look like a railroad station. Train schedules were posted and empty buildings that looked like stores could be seen. Deportees to Treblinka were greeted with the following sign:

> Attention, Warsaw Jews! You are in a transit camp from which the transport will continue to labor camps. To prevent epidemics, clothing as well as pieces of baggage are to be handed over for disinfection. Gold, money, foreign currency, and jewelry are to

be deposited at the "Cash Office" [and a receipt will be given]. They will be returned later on presentation of the receipt. For physical cleanliness, all arrivals must have a bath before travelling on.[17]

Whether the Warsaw Jews believed the deception mattered little. Knowingly or unknowingly, they were led to their deaths. One of the few survivors, Abraham Goldfarb, saw the same horrible scene over and over:

> **"To escape from the blows, the victims ran to the gas chambers as quickly as they could . . ."**

On the way to the gas chambers Germans with dogs stood along the fence on both sides. The dogs had been trained to attack people; they bit the men's genitals and the women's breasts, ripping off pieces of flesh. The Germans hit the people with whips and iron bars to spur them on so that they pressed forward into the "showers" as quickly as possible. The screams of the women could be heard far away, even in the other parts of the camp. The Germans drove the running victims on with shouts of: "Faster, faster, the water will get cold, others still have to go under the showers!" To escape from the blows, the victims ran to the gas chambers as quickly as they could, the stronger ones pushing the weaker aside. At the entrance to the gas chambers stood the two Ukrainians, Ivan Demaniuk and Nikolai . . . one of them

> armed with an iron bar, the other with a sword. They drove the people inside with blows. . . . As soon as the gas chambers were full, the Ukrainians closed the doors and started the engine.[18]

Each of the ten gas chambers at Treblinka could hold about two hundred people. But in July 1942, hundreds of thousands of Jews were still alive and Hitler's armies were bogged down in the Soviet Union. Perhaps concerned that the war might end before all of Europe's Jews could be killed, Himmler issued an order: The murder of all the Jews in occupied Poland must be completed by December 31. New, larger gas chambers were built at Treblinka, and gas chambers were installed in two labor camps.

Majdanek

In the work camp of Majdanek, outside the city of Lublin, shower facilities were converted to gas chambers. Even before Majdanek became a death camp, thousands of inmates had died from the brutal work, starvation, disease, and the sadism of the guards. Any who appeared too weak to work were disposed of upon arrival. When the Jews began to be deported to Majdanek, a very few were selected for work and the rest were either shot or gassed. Young children were of no use in the camp, so they were killed immediately. Nechamah Epstein, barely twenty, was one of the few allowed to live:

> We were taken off at the Majdanek lager [camp]. We were all lined up. There were many who were shot. . . . Everything was separated. The women, the young women, were sent to the Majdanek lager. The men were

YOUTH DESTROYED—THE NAZI CAMPS

In Majdanek, the shower rooms were converted into gas chambers. The interior of a gas chamber at Majdanek is shown in this photo after the camp was liberated. The blue stain is from the Zyklon B, the poison used to kill the victims.

> taken to another lager. The children and the mothers were led to the crematorium. . . . We never laid eyes on them again.[19]

Older youth were often spared. Abraham Lewent, at nineteen, must have looked strong. But he learned painfully how important maintaining his strength was:

> We were standing in a ditch and digging, and my father was standing next to me. A [Gentile prisoner] grabs a stone and throws it onto my father. . . . The stone hit his leg. I don't know what happened, if he broke a bone or something happened. He couldn't walk. . . . Somehow we dragged him, me and that friend, we dragged him in the barrack. . . . And his foot swelled up. . . . Well, I didn't realize what's going to happen if somebody gets sick. . . . The medic came. He . . . took my father. He says to him, "You know what? You have to go [to] the hospital. And he took him away. And he says tomorrow he's going to bring him back. I never saw my father anymore.[20]

At least 80,000 prisoners who entered Majdanek were killed there. At Chelmno, 152,000 were killed; at Belzec, 434,500; at Treblinka, 870,000; and at Sobibor, at least 167,000. The largest of all the camps, Auschwitz, claimed the lives of 1.1 million.[21]

Chapter Five

AUSCHWITZ

Auschwitz was established in 1940 as a concentration camp for Polish political prisoners. It was gradually expanded to consist of three main camps and over forty subcamps. The first facility was called Auschwitz I. There, and at Auschwitz III, also called Buna or Monowitz, prisoners toiled at one of the factories installed by German companies such as I. G. Farben and Krupps Steel. In March 1942, a building at Auschwitz II-Birkenau was converted into a gas chamber, and Auschwitz II soon functioned as an annihilation camp. So Auschwitz, the largest of all the camps, was a prison, labor, and death camp.

Learning the Truth

The mass killings at the camp began in July 1942. Many of the Jews, like twelve-year-old David Bergman who arrived in 1944, did not know what awaited them:

> We arrived . . . in the morning. It was a nice day. We were all with anticipation. Where are we heading? Then the train . . . kept slowing down, and . . . we see barbed wire compound there. . . . All of a sudden, the train came to a stop. And they opened the doors. That was when I saw Hell.
> We were forced to get out. All of a sudden, I saw Nazis beating people . . . dragging children away from their parents

> . . . parents trying to go after children. And you hear shooting and yelling and crying and children. . . . Fear took over me. What is this all about? What's happening? What are we doing here? This is not a city in Hungary. This is not what we had thought.[1]

Seventeen-year-old Kate Bernath was equally surprised:

> We didn't know what Auschwitz was or where we were. . . . They opened the doors [of the cattle cars] and these men with striped uniforms started to drag us out and the Germans patrolling with their German Shepherd [dogs] and yelling, " . . . Schnell, schnell [hurry, hurry]!" Everything has to be done "schnell" all the time. As soon as we got off, they threw [our backpacks] all out on the side, and we didn't need it anymore actually, but we didn't know that. And men and women were separated right away. Separate lines. . . . We had no idea of what was waiting for us.[2]

Some began to get an idea when they saw the weakest of the new arrivals being separated from the rest. Sixteen-year-old Helen Lebowitz watched in horror:

> You see these mothers coming down with little kids, and they're trying to pull these kids out of their mother's hands. And, you know, when you try to separate a family, it's very difficult. . . . People put up fights. . . . There was so much screams. So, there was a truck. . . . The parents, the mothers that wouldn't give up

these children . . . were beaten up, and
the kids got hurt. So they grabbed these
kids and they threw them on the truck,
and they really didn't look how they were
throwing them on the truck. So at that time
we saw that something horrible is happening—
the way these people were behaving to
little children, to little babies. And
. . . on that truck . . . they were
throwing sick people . . . and these
children that gave them a tough time. They
were just thrown on the trucks. And there
were so many mothers that were running
after the trucks,
and of course they
beat them and they
pushed them back.³

Leo Schneiderman's mother figured it all out moments after she and her sons arrived:

When we came in,
the minute the gate
opened up, we heard
screams, barking
of dogs, blows from
. . . Kapos, those
officials working
for them. . . . And
everything went so
fast: left, right,
right, left. Men
separated from
women. Children

After the "selection" process, those Jews chosen for work received prison uniforms. This striped skirt was part of a prison uniform worn by women at Auschwitz-Birkenau.

> torn from the arms of mothers. The elderly chased like cattle. The sick, the disabled were handled like packs of garbage. They were thrown in a side together with broken suitcases, with boxes. My mother ran over to me and grabbed me by the shoulders, and she told me, "Leibele, I'm not going to see you no more. Take care of your brother."[4]

What every Jew who entered Auschwitz learned was that it was a facility for mass murder. The camp's commandant, Rudolf Höss, testified that it was designed to kill many people at once:

> The "final solution" of the Jewish question meant the complete extermination of all Jews in Europe. I was ordered to establish extermination facilities at Auschwitz. . . . [An] improvement we made over Treblinka was that we built our gas chambers to accommodate two thousand people at one time, whereas at Treblinka their ten gas chambers only accommodated two hundred people each.[5]

"Selection"

When the gas chambers were ready, workers were still needed for the Nazi war industries. And Auschwitz was a huge labor camp. Therefore, every time the trains brought more Jews, a "selection" had to be made: Who would work and who would die?

Höss described the decision-making process:

> We had two SS doctors on duty at Auschwitz to examine the incoming transports of prisoners. The prisoners would be marched by one of the doctors, who would make spot

> decisions as they walked by. Those who were fit for work were sent into the camp. Others were sent immediately to the extermination plants. Children of tender years were invariably exterminated since by reason of their youth they were unable to work.[6]

Höss tried to keep the selection process calm and orderly, but that was not always possible:

> At Auschwitz we endeavored to fool the victims into thinking that they were to go through a delousing process. Of course, frequently they realized our true intentions and we sometimes had riots and difficulties due to that fact. Very frequently women would hide their children under the clothes, but of course when we found them we would send the children in to be exterminated. We were required to carry out these exterminations in secrecy, but of course the foul and nauseating stench from the continuous burning of bodies permeated the entire area.[7]

Of all the SS doctors, the most hated was Josef Mengele. When Abraham Malach faced this man, later dubbed the "Angel of Death," he was only nine. Years later, he remembered:

> The infamous Dr. Mengele, he would stand at the head of the column of the procession of naked people and some way before reaching, coming up in front of Mengele, we saw that there's left and there's right. . . . People would march up in front of him and

AUSCHWITZ

Rudolf Höss (right), Josef Mengele (center), and Richard Baer stand together in July 1944. Mengele was later dubbed the "Angel of Death." Höss served as camp commandant until November 1943. Richard Baer took over the position in May 1944.

```
he would look at them and whether they are
still able bodied or not, able to contribute
toward the work, to the labor in the
factories. So when my turn came, and
somebody was whispering to me, "To the
right." And somehow I managed to stay in
that right lane without being motioned back
to the left lane. That's what made the
difference of life and death.[8]
```

Malach was more fortunate than most children. The Nazis considered anyone under fourteen unable to work. Some, like David Bergman, survived the selection by lying about their age:

We heard orders, barking: "That line! That line! That line!" And I found myself in a line with other youth. I had no idea which line we were supposed to be [in]. . . . I was looking for my father, you see, because there were all men on one side. I ran out from the group of youth that I was in, and I ran towards the adults. That's what actually saved my life. . . . And then my turn came. . . . [The Nazi officer] asked me how old I was. My voice just froze. For some reason, something within me said, "Don't say anything."

He kept saying, "How old are you?"

. . . [My father] said I'm fourteen. . . . [The Nazi officer] looked at me kind of suspiciously. . . . "Fourteen?" And in a split second said, "Okay, you can go with the work group." I kept wanting to say, "No. No, Dad. I'm only twelve." Something held me back. If I would have said twelve, that would have been it.[9]

> "I ran out from the group of youth that I was in, and I ran towards the adults. That's what actually saved my life."

Other Jewish prisoners at the camp saved Fritzie Weiss. By Nazi standards, she was not old enough to work:

The train arrived in the middle of the night, so we were greeted by very bright lights shining down on us. We were greeted by soldiers, SS men, as well as women. We were greeted by dogs and whips, by shouting and screaming, orders to try to empty the train, by confusion, and by men in striped uniform. We didn't know it at the time, but the men in uniform were the Jews who were brought there before us. . . . Their job was to empty the train. . . . Those men would come onto the . . . train and they would try and push and pull us off the train as fast as they could. These men were not allowed to speak to us, but in their own way they tried to help young people. They walked amongst us and in Yiddish would whisper to a child, "You're fifteen. Remember, you're fifteen." When we got off the train, they asked us to line up according to age. I lined up and I became fifteen years old.[10]

Induction Into the Labor Camp

Weiss, Malach, Bergman, and all the other "adults" were destined for the factories, the kitchens, the clothes-sorting rooms, and other work details. First, they were stripped of the few belongings they had left. Edgar Krasa, barely out of his teens, recalled:

We were brought to a huge hall, with nothing in [it] except benches around, and pegs on the wall. The pegs were numbered, and we were told to take everything off and hang it on a peg and remember the number so you can get back to your clothes. Till the last moment were deceptions. [The SS said,] "And everything you have in your pocket. There's a blanket on the ground—throw out everything . . . and don't let us find anything on you. You'll get severely punished."[11]

Edgar Krasa poses in a kitchen sometime between 1940 and 1941. Krasa experienced the horrible process of going into the Auschwitz labor camp.

When they had nothing left but their bare naked bodies, Krasa remembered, the Nazis took even more: "Then we were shaved, every hair on our body. . . . They never changed the blade—that was dull. They were pulling the hair and ripping the skin. And after that, we were washed down with some disinfectant that burned in those scratches."[12]

The prisoners' hair was shorn for two reasons. It was made into felt and yarn for socks for German sailors. Its absence would slow the spread of lice. The shaving was especially humiliating for young girls such as Carola Steinhardt:

> I was seventeen, so I was sent into the [labor] camp. . . . In the sauna, they cut our hair. . . . We were all sitting together, not knowing each other because we had no hair and . . . for a young girl to suddenly have no hair whatsoever was a devastating experience. But it wasn't the worst. . . . We went in a line. Some of them did their head and some of them did the other—you know, bodily hairs.[13]

The newcomers were given new identities—or rather, their identities were taken from them. People like Steinhardt and Krasa no longer had names, but numbers. As another step in the dehumanization process, the Nazis tattooed numbers on the forearms of their Jewish prisoners. The final preparation of the prisoners for work, Krasa recalled, was clothing them:

> Hot water, nice showering, after three days in filth. There was no food the three days, and we still were not eating before the shower. And [we were] not coming back to the peg [where we had hung our clothes], but another door. They chased us out, naked and wet from a hot shower in the cold, wintry night to another barrack. And then we're marching along a counter, behind which some prisoners were sitting and throwing at us a pair of pants, a jacket, and a pair of boots. And the . . . cap to take off when you meet an SS man—it was for no other reason. . . . That clothing was without regard to our size, so it was up to us then to exchange it so it fits.[14]

Bales of human hair, weighing more than fifteen thousand pounds, found in one of the Auschwitz warehouses after liberation of the camp. The Nazis shaved the prisoners' hair so it could be made into felt and yarn for the German war effort.

Periodic Selections

For the Jews of Auschwitz, work was only temporary. The cruel conditions would soon sap their strength and they would be sent to the gas chambers. New prisoners would take their place. The inmates were lined up regularly and made to walk in front of the camp "doctors." Any children who had escaped the first selection when they came into the camp were especially vulnerable each time there was a new selection. Some, like nine-year-old Ruth Webber, were fortunate:

> One of the selections that were going on, I was hidden with other children in a hole in the ground where they kept potatoes, right off the kitchen. And we were there up until the point when they were putting the people on the trucks. Already, the selections have been made. And somebody must have [seen] us going in there, and they had told one of the Germans. And there was potatoes lying over us so we were actually hidden, but somebody told him exactly where we are. So he came up and he uncovered us. He pulled up all these potatoes away, and he looked at us—there was a few of us there. And he said—he was there with his handgun—and he said, "Stay here. It's not safe for you to come out yet." I guess he had enough people for this particular transport, so he had a change of heart and he decided to leave us there. We were children, so we ran out. My mother was working in the kitchen peeling potatoes and she saw me coming, so a couple of the ladies and my mother grabbed me and put me into a barrel with sauerkraut in it

until the trucks were pulled away. And I was saved that time.[15]

Medical Experimentation

Other children were also saved from death in the gas chambers, but not from torture. Josef Mengele, the camp doctor who conducted many selections, performed medical experiments on some of the inmates. He was particularly fascinated with twins because he thought he could learn more about genetics by studying them. Unlocking secrets of genetics might enable him to perfect the "master race." Eva Moses was nine when she and her sister became two of Mengele's twins: "We were always naked during the experiments. We were marked, painted, measured, observed. . . . It was all so demeaning. There was no place to hide, no place to go. They compared every part of our body with that of our twin. The tests would last for hours."[16]

Thirteen-year-old Hedvah and Leah Stern remembered the experiments as painful, frightening, and humiliating:

> Mengele was trying to change the color of our eyes. One day, we were given eye-drops. Afterwards, we could not see for several days. We thought the Nazis had made us blind. We were very frightened of the experiments. They took a lot of blood from us. We fainted several times. . . . The Nazis made us remove our clothes, and then they took photographs of us. . . . We stood naked in front of these young Nazi thugs, shaking from cold and fear, and they laughed.[17]

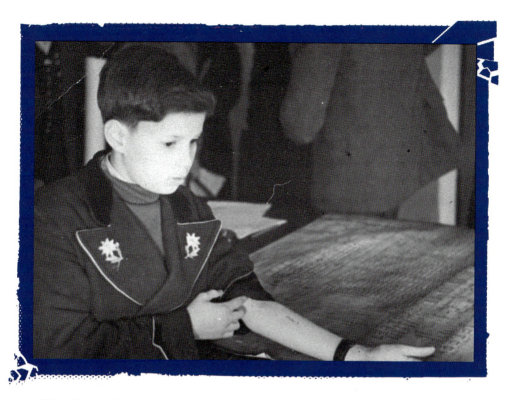

The Nazis further dehumanized their victims by giving them numbers tattooed on their arms. Luigi Ferri, a child survivor of Auschwitz, shows his tattoo (B7525) after liberation.

The twins experiments and other atrocities continued through most of 1944. By the summer, however, Germany was losing the war. Soviet troops were advancing through Poland and the Nazis feared the camps would be discovered. They began sending inmates to camps in Germany. In July, the Soviet army liberated Majdanek.

Auschwitz, however, was much more than a death camp. With its constellation of subcamps, it was a huge weapons factory that "employed" thousands of workers. Himmler resisted shutting down the very large and productive operation. But as the Soviet troops drew closer, he had no choice. In November 1944, the last gassing took place. The Nazis dismantled the gas chambers. What would they do with the prisoners?

In the final, chaotic days of the camp, they killed as many as they could. In January 1945, they gave the order for the sixty thousand who remained to march west, toward Germany. By this time, almost no children were left at the camp, but some teens were among the adults on the death marches. They trudged more than thirty miles through rain and snow, clad in their thin prison garb. Then they were transported in unheated railroad cars to camps in Germany. Fifteen thousand died on the death marches.

When the Soviet soldiers liberated Auschwitz on January 27, 1945, they found 7,650 prisoners, all barely alive. In its four and a half years of operation, at least 1.3 million prisoners were brought to the camp. The camp personnel killed an estimated 1.1 million of them.[18]

Chapter Six

AFTER THE CAMPS

By the summer of 1943, the inmates of the camps understood all too well what was happening. Most realized they were all marked for death. Some decided to resist. Inmates in their teens were instrumental in several of the revolts, including uprisings at three death camps: Sobibor, Treblinka, and Auschwitz. Sixteen-year-old Thomas Blatt was a part of the resistance at Sobibor:

> I was a young kid; I shouldn't be involved in the organization direct but I was involved for two reasons. Because I was the boss . . . of the place where they burned the papers and this was a place where a German could easy be called in and killed and nobody will see it. And [one of the leaders] knew me very well. . . . There was a few of us young people who was able to move about more easier than the grown-up people.[1]

In Treblinka, the youngest in the camp could also move about with a little less suspicion. Twenty-one-year-old Kalman Teigman observed that the revolt there would not have been possible without the help of children:

> Two children of the Hofjuden [children with special privileges] were employed in

> polishing the shoes of the Germans, and
> they worked in the hut where there was an
> arms store. This store was built by the
> experts amongst the Hofjuden, the fitters
> and the construction workers. An extra key
> to the store had to be made. And, in fact
> they made a key, and the children were to
> go into the store, to remove arms in sacks,
> and to place them on refuse carts—guns,
> bullets, hand grenades and revolvers.[2]

At Auschwitz, the Sonderkommando, realizing they were about to be killed, destroyed a crematorium and killed three guards. They used explosives supplied by young women who worked at an armaments factory at the camp. Anna Heilmann, age sixteen, was part of the planning:

> It began this way. A small group of
> girls were getting together after work
> in Auschwitz dreaming of Israel, singing
> Hebrew songs and talking about life outside,
> or in the future, if we survive. . . . We,
> too, decided that we were not going to let
> ourselves be taken without a struggle. . . .
> We were about seven or eight girls, no
> more. Out of this friendship evolved the
> ideas of resistance. . . . What could we
> do, each one of us, to resist?[3]

The resistance attempts were very small successes. Only a handful of camp guards were killed. Of the few hundred who escaped, most were later recaptured and shot. All the prisoners who were involved in the plotting—and many who were not—were executed. But the rebellions, coming at the same time as the number of German military defeats was growing, hastened the closure of the camps. The Nazis began the process of closing the camps after the uprisings: Sobibor and Treblinka in the Fall of 1943 and Auschwitz in November 1944.

Death Marches

By early 1944, Soviet troops were closing in on the eastern front, and Himmler was worried that the remaining camps would be discovered. Chelmno and Belzec had already been dismantled. But Majdanek, Auschwitz, and a number of forced labor camps were still in operation. Himmler ordered the easternmost camps to be closed and all evidence of their grisly work destroyed. The prisoners who were still alive were marched to camps in

> "We, too, decided that we were not going to let ourselves be taken without a struggle."

the west, away from the liberating army. Fritzie Weiss was sixteen when her forced march from Auschwitz began:

> [We] started the death march. . . . All of us were weak already. . . . We did not know where we were going to go, but we knew that it was the last days of the war. We knew because of the bombings, and we knew because of the way the German soldiers were pushing us and pulling us already and emptying the camps and whatever. They took us all and put us together, all of the people from camps, and they had us march through towns and through fields. They didn't know where to put us anymore and

YOUTH DESTROYED—THE NAZI CAMPS

> they didn't know what to do with us and there was no food because the Germans were losing the war. Oftentimes as they marched us through a town, a window would open and a shutter would open and either a potato or a loaf of bread would come flying out and the shutter would close after. And we would all pounce on this potato or . . . this piece of food that came at us. And of course they would shoot at us, but we didn't care at that point because we were hungry. The streets were literally covered with bodies as we marched. We would pass bodies, body after body after body, people that were dropping dead from hunger, from disease, from dysentery, because they did not have the strength or because they gave up. So we knew it was toward the end.[4]

Lilly Appelbaum, a year older than Weiss, also knew when she left Auschwitz that the end of the war was near:

> Word came to us that we were going to evacuate Auschwitz. Why were we evacuating Auschwitz? It is because the Russians were coming close by. And so we all walked out [of] Auschwitz and we started walking. . . . We walked for days. I'll never forget it. I don't know how many days we walked. We walked and then we took cattle cars and then we walked again.[5]

Neither the walking, the weakness, nor the hunger was the worst part of the death marches. The worst part, as Appelbaum remembered, was the shooting:

AFTER THE CAMPS

Prisoners in Auschwitz greet their liberators sometime after January 27, 1945. Most of the remaining inmates in Auschwitz had been forced to leave on a death march. When the camp was liberated, only 7,650 prisoners were still there.

As we walked we heard gun shots and they told us to keep on marching. . . . They were shooting people in the back who couldn't keep up with the walking. It ended up being called the death march because the ravines and the gutters, they were all red from blood. . . . Some people who thought they could escape would try and escape. Some people who couldn't keep up with the walking anymore, they got weak, they threw all their bundles away and they walked until they couldn't keep up anymore. They fell behind and the Germans just shot them. We saw people being shot in the front in their chests, in their back. They were laying all over, on top of hills, behind trees. It was really like a war zone.[6]

> "They fell behind and the Germans just shot them. We saw people being shot in the front in their chests, in their back."

As the Allied armies began liberating one camp after another, the skeletal inmates kept marching farther west. They walked in the rain and the snow, often for twelve hours at a stretch, day after day, without food or water. Weiss focused on staying alive: "We would sleep in the fields. We lived on whatever we could find. If we could find a carrot, a potato, snails—snails! In order to survive. The planes would come down low and shoot at us often times."[7]

Lily Mazur, twenty-one when evacuated from the labor camp at Stutthof, tried to help prisoners who were not as strong as she:

> We knew the only way we can survive if we will stay in the front. Because if you were standing in the back and you couldn't walk with the column, you were just shot. And then I saw young girls walk and walk, and all of a sudden they became like frozen—straightened their legs instead, and they were just frozen mummies falling right with their face on the snow. The German didn't have to shoot them. This is how they fell. One of my friends started to feel bad, and we took her, and I was from one side, and another of my friend, and we were dragging her, practically dragging her. She couldn't—her legs were frozen. So the guard noticed it. He told the column to stop. He took her to a turnip field, and we heard a shot. He shot her right there.[8]

By April 1945, much of Germany was in Allied hands. There were still thousands of prisoners and no camp left to put them. Sam Itzkowitz was twenty when he was evacuated from Landsberg, a subcamp of Dachau in Germany:

> They decided to march us towards the Bavarian mountains, to the Alps. 'Til today I don't know what the reason was. Either they wanted to destroy us in those mountains or they were going to trade us off through Switzerland. There was the death march. Well, I was already so weak that I could barely walk. That march [took] ten days to two weeks. Snow in the daytime, snow at night. . . . And we had to sleep outside. . . . They always camped us out somewhere in an open field. And we just

huddled together like animals in the street, in the wilderness. And just tried to stay alive. And on top of it we saw planes coming over us. . . . And we were praying, hoping, we says, "Come on, drop them, get it over with." . . . I think the pilots saw that we were prisoners and they dropped bombs all around us, but never on us. See, we were wearing those striped uniforms.[9]

Freedom

Despite the bombing and the guards with guns, some managed to escape their Nazi captors during the death marches. Fritzie Weiss was one:

Towards the very last, a friend . . . and I ran into the forest. I believe they saw us run. I believe the Germans saw us run because they could have shot us at that point. But they didn't. We ran into the forest and spent the first night in the forest sleeping. And we spent all the next day there because we were afraid to go out. And when it started to get dark, she and I found a town to walk to. And we came to a farmer. And, of course, they had to know who we were. Our heads were shaved and we wore striped clothing. And we begged for food and they did give us food and told us to go into the barn. . . . And when the man left, we ran out of the barn and ran away because we were afraid they would turn us in. And we lived in the forests until the Russians liberated us.[10]

AFTER THE CAMPS

An enormous pile of victims' shoes was found outside barracks at the Dachau concentration camp after the camp was liberated.

The Russians liberated some camps, and the British and the Americans liberated others. Most of the liberating soldiers had no idea that they were freeing emaciated civilians. They were still fighting a war. Harry Herder was a nineteen-year-old private in the U.S. Army when his unit entered Buchenwald on April 11, 1945. With guns ready, the unit's tanks barreled through three barbed-wire fences. Herder recalled:

> Just inside of the [last] fence, and to our front, were some major buildings, and next to one of those buildings was a monster of a chimney. . . . Black smoke was pouring out of it, and blowing away from us, but we could still smell it. An ugly,

101

> horrible smell. A vicious smell. . . .
> We were fully expecting a fire fight with
> German troops, whose camp we had just
> stormed and taken, and we thought they
> would be angry at us. It turned out there
> were no German troops present.[11]

The Germans had fled, but that was only the first surprise for Herder. The battles he had fought had not prepared him for what he saw next:

> Slowly . . . a ragged group of human beings
> started to creep out of and from between
> the buildings in front of us . . . timidly,
> slowly, deliberately showing their hands,
> all in a sort of uniform, or bits and
> pieces of a uniform, made from horribly
> coarse cloth with stripes. . . . They came
> out of the buildings and just stood there,
> making me feel foolish with all of that
> firepower hanging on me. . . . Hesitatingly
> we inched closer to that strange group as
> they also started inching closer to us.
> Some of them spoke English, and asked, "Are
> you American?" We said we were, and the
> reaction of the whole mass was immediate:
> simultaneously on their faces were
> relaxation, ease, joy, and they all began
> chattering to us in a babble of tongues
> that we couldn't answer. . . . We hadn't
> the vaguest idea what we had run into. . . .
> We still had no idea what this place was.[12]

Herder learned quickly about Buchenwald. When he walked beyond the buildings, he came upon a sight he would remember for the rest of his life:

AFTER THE CAMPS

Mauthausen survivors cheer the soldiers of the Eleventh Armored Division of the U.S. Third Army one day after their liberation. Soldiers from the armies who liberated the camps often could not believe what they saw.

```
The bodies of human beings were stacked
like cord wood. All of them dead. All of
them stripped. . . . The stack was about
five feet high, maybe a little more. . . .
They extended down the hill, only a slight
hill, for fifty to seventy-five feet. Human
bodies neatly stacked, naked, ready for
disposal. . . . There was an aisle, then
another stack, and another aisle, and
more stacks. The Lord only knows how many
there were.[13]
```

YOUTH DESTROYED—THE NAZI CAMPS

The liberators turned their attention from the dead to the living. Many of the freed prisoners met their liberators with cheers and tears. Many others were too weak to even smile. Bela Braver described the liberation of Auschwitz:

> The camp guard who came to open the gate said, "You are free and you can leave." All the guards with the dogs that used to stand in every corner had disappeared. It was all gone, as though it had never been. It was one of the miracles! The Russians entered, and we were in such a condition that no one moved, no one went out. We did not laugh, we were not happy, we were apathetic—and the Russians came. A general came in, he was Jewish. He told us that he was delighted, as this was the first camp in which he found people still alive. He started to cry; but we didn't. He wept and we didn't.[14]

Freedom was bittersweet for the children of the camps. Many had lost all their relatives. Those who still had family members living did not know where they were or how to find them. They had no homes to which to return. Eva Braun had mixed feelings when she and her sister were liberated from Auschwitz:

> While I was elated by the freedom, there was tremendous fear. Who would I find? We had survived this but we now have to go back to civilization. How would we react in a normal world again? We were two young girls without anything. Who will take care of us? What will we do? It was euphoria,

AFTER THE CAMPS

After liberation, many children had no homes to return to and no way to find their surviving relatives. Thousands of Jewish children ended up in DP camps. These girls are playing in the snow at the Kloster Indersdorf DP children's center on February 14, 1946.

```
but it was a very ambivalent feeling. We
were frightened.[15]
```

The Allies and the United Nations (UN) set up displaced persons (DP) camps where victims of the Nazis could live while they put their lives back together. Fela Warschau, nineteen when liberated from Bergen-Belsen, went to a DP camp near Munich:

```
We had the clothes which we wore there,
which was full of disease and lice. . . .
They gave us different clothes. . . . We
were all happy just to be alive and be
liberated. . . . Reading the lists from
```

> other camps—from the survivors that lived through this—[that is] what kept me going. . . . But when I didn't find anybody . . . I caved in. I only lived with that hope that I will meet my family.[16]

Only three of Warschau's sixty relatives survived.

Two members of Thomas Buergenthal's family were alive after the war, but the eleven-year-old had no way of knowing that. He lived in an orphanage for three years before, as he said, "Something unbelievable happened":

> My mother had survived the camp, and my . . . mother's brother. . . . They began looking for me all over, of course, after the war. And they couldn't find me. My mother never gave up hope that I was alive. Everybody told her it's impossible that he survived. But she believed that I survived. And . . . somebody . . . noticed that there was a child in the orphanage in Poland who . . . met the description of the child that the woman was looking for in Germany, and notified my uncle . . . and that's how I was eventually reunited with my mother.[17]

Lasting Effects

The children who lived through the Holocaust camps eventually grew up. Most of them found jobs, married, and had families. They led normal lives. But many were forever scarred by the camp experience. Some lived with permanent health problems and some battled fears. Dr. Irene Butter, fifteen when the war ended, had wept so many times as the trains carried away her loved ones.

AFTER THE CAMPS

This wedding dress was made from an old German parachute. Lily Lax Friedman wore it first on her wedding day on January 27, 1946. Another seventeen to twenty young brides wore the dress in the Celle and Belsen DP camps. The survivors of the Holocaust had to start their lives over after the war and many did that beginning in the DP camps.

She became a successful college professor, but forty years after liberation, she still cried: "I have never been able to get over it, because I have this reaction whenever I see a train, I still do. It's just somehow a part of me; there is something about trains that I have never been able to overcome."[18]

Ellen Levi survived four camps by the age of fifteen by trying not to feel. She carried that hardness with her the rest of her life:

> I think I suppressed all emotions, otherwise I could not survive. I saw people dying, I saw the furnace of the crematorium. And I suppressed feelings; I had to. . . . I suppressed feelings about the trains. I did not want to think about where they were going. I knew fear, but I really didn't know, and I preferred not to know. And this suppression of feelings continued afterward, it continues, yes, for a long, long time. It continues [today].[19]

"I saw people dying, I saw the furnace of the crematorium. And I suppressed feelings."

Many of the children of the camps endured such unspeakable horrors that they could not even voice their experiences. A woman named Bronia, who was sent to Auschwitz when she was twelve and saw her siblings perish there, did not tell her husband or her children that she ever had brothers or sisters. "For 50 years," she said, "I was not able to say a word about it. . . . I felt totally constricted, a choking feeling. It took me 25 years to be able to laugh."[20]

AFTER THE CAMPS

After many years, Bronia and other children of the Holocaust have found their voice. They are telling their stories. Alice Lok Cahana, the fifteen-year-old girl who escaped death when the Auschwitz Sonderkommando blew up a crematorium, explained why: "All of us who survived took a silent oath, made a promise to tell a glimpse of the story. Not to let the world forget."[21]

Not to let the world forget. That is why courageous people are reliving painful memories. That is why this book was written—so they could tell a glimpse of their stories. Not to let the world forget.

CHART OF CAMP DEATHS

Camp	Opened	Closed	Time in Operation	No. Killed (at least)
Chelmno	December 8, 1941	April 7, 1943 6/23/44–7/14/44 reopened January 17, 1945 evacuated	17 mos.	152,000
Belzec	March 17, 1942	June 1943	15 mos.	434,500
Sobibor	April 1942	October 14, 1943 revolt, Nazis dismantle	17 mos.	167,000
Treblinka	July 23, 1942	August 2, 1943 revolt Fall 1943 Nazis dismantle camp II July 1944 Nazis shoot remaining prisoners at camp I and evacuate	16 mos.	870,000
Majdanek	October 1941 POW camp December 1941 forced labor camp October 1942 death camp	April 1944 to June 1944 Nazis evacuate July 24, 1944 liberated	32 mos.	80,000
Auschwitz	June 14, 1940 prison camp February 1942 death camp	October 7, 1944 revolt November 25, 1944 gas chambers destroyed January 18, 1945 evacuated January 27, 1945 liberated	56 mos.	1,100,000
			Total killed in death camps	2,803,500

TIMELINE

1933

January 30—Adolf Hitler becomes chancellor of Germany.

March 22—The first major concentration camp is opened at Dachau.

1936

July 12—Concentration camp Sachsenhausen is opened in Germany.

1937

July 15—Concentration camp Buchenwald is opened in Germany.

1938

May—Concentration camp Flossenbürg is opened in Germany.

August 8—Concentration camp Mauthausen is opened in Austria.

November 9–10—*Kristallnacht*, Nazi-instigated attack on Jewish shops and homes, known as the "Night of Broken Glass," ends with arrest of more than thirty thousand Jewish males and their internment in concentration camps.

YOUTH DESTROYED—THE NAZI CAMPS

1939
May 15—Ravensbrück near Berlin begins operation as first concentration camp primarily for women.
September 1—German invasion of Poland begins World War II.

1940
May 10—Germany invades France; Paris falls June 14; an armistice is signed June 22.
June 14—Concentration camp Auschwitz is opened in Poland.

1941
April—Danica concentration camp is established in Croatia (Yugoslavia).
May—Natzweiler concentration camp is built in eastern France.
June 22—Germany invades Russia.
Late 1941—Labor and POW camp Majdanek is opened in Poland.
December 8—Death camp Chelmno is opened.

1942
January 20—Wannsee Conference discusses the "final solution."
February—Auschwitz is designated a death camp.
March 17—Death camp Belzec is opened.

TIMELINE

May—Death camp Sobibor is opened.
July 23—Death camp Treblinka II is opened.
End of 1942—Gas chambers are installed at Majdanek.

1943

April—The SS closes Chelmno (although reopened in 1944 for four months).
June—Belzec is closed.
August 2—Revolt at Treblinka; SS destroys camp in November.
October 14—Revolt at Sobibor; SS destroys camp in December.

1944

July 24—Majdanek, first camp to be liberated, is liberated by Russian army.
October 7—Revolt at Auschwitz destroys one crematorium.

1945

January 18—Evacuation of Auschwitz begins.
April 30—Hitler commits suicide.
May 5–8—Mauthausen, last camp to be liberated, is liberated by U.S. Army.
May 8, 1945—Germany surrenders unconditionally, ending World War II.

CHAPTER NOTES

Introduction

1. Alice Lok Cahana, "Selection in Auschwitz," excerpt from *Empty Windows and Now in Auschwitz Flowers Grow: The Art and Writings of Alice Lok Cahana*, n.d., <http://www.albany.edu/museum/wwwmuseum/holo/Cahana.htm> (November 18, 2008).
2. Alice Lok Cahana, interview with Barbara Rose, *Women Artists of the American West*, n.d., <http://www.cla.purdue.edu/WAAW/Ressler/artists/cahanabio.html> (November 18, 2008).
3. Alice Lok Cahana, "Describes arrival at Bergen-Belsen," USHMM, interview 1990, <http://www.ushmm.org/museum/exhibit/online/phistories/viewmedia/phi_fset.php?MediaId=1081> (August 28, 2009).
4. Martin Gilbert, *Routledge Atlas of the Holocaust*, 3rd ed. (New York: Routledge, 2002), p. 11.

Chapter 1. The Concentration Camps

1. Golly D., cited in Joshua M. Greene and Shiva Kumar, eds., *Witness: Voices from the Holocaust* (New York: Free Press, 2000), p. 4.
2. Ibid., p. 14.
3. Vera Dahl, cited in Martin Gilbert, *Kristallnacht: Prelude to Destruction* (New York: HarperCollins, 2006), p. 76.
4. Rita Newell Braumann, cited in Gilbert, pp. 78–79.
5. Laurie Lowenthal, "My Childhood in Germany," typescript sent to Martin Gilbert, cited in Gilbert, p. 30.
6. Lea Weems, cited in Gilbert, pp. 113–114.
7. Cited in Mark Jonathan Harris and Deborah Oppenheimer, *Into the Arms of Strangers: Stories of the Kindertransport* (New York: MJF Books, 2000), pp. 69, 71.
8. Theodore Haas, interview, "Jews in the Dachau Camp," June 12, 2007, <http://www.scrapbookpages.com/DachauScrapbook/KZDachau/DachauLife4.html> (December 3, 2008).
9. Ibid.
10. Harris and Oppenheimer, p. 75.

CHAPTER NOTES

11. Leo Kutner, "Stutthof," United States Holocaust Memorial Museum (USHMM), n.d., <http://www.ushmm.org/wlc/media_oi.php?lang=en&ModuleId=10005197&MediaId=1169> (October 24, 2008).
12. Bela Blau, Oral History Transcript, USHMM Archives RG-50.030*0029.
13. Harris and Oppenheimer, p. 45.

Chapter 2. Waiting Rooms

1. Peter Ernst Feigl, Oral History Transcript, United States Holocaust Memorial Museum (USHMM) Archives RG-50.030*0272.
2. Ibid.
3. Hanne Hirsch Liebmann, "Gurs," USHMM, n.d., <http://www.ushmm.org/wlc/media_oi.php?lang=en&ModuleId=10005298&MediaId=1652> (October 24, 2008).
4. Eva Lang, cited in "Camp of Rivesaltes," *Jewish Traces*, n.d., <http://www.jewishtraces.org/rubriques/?keyRubrique=camp_of_rivesaltes> (December 8, 2008).
5. Max Karl Liebmann, "Gurs," USHMM, n.d., <http://www.ushmm.org/wlc/media_oi.php?lang=en&ModuleId=10005298&MediaId=2361> (October 24, 2008).
6. Cited in Susan Zuccotti, *The Holocaust, the French, and the Jews* (New York: HarperCollins, 1994), pp. 81–82.
7. Ibid., p. 82.
8. Ibid.
9. Ernest Koenig, Oral History Transcript, USHMM Archives, RG-50.030*0112.
10. Leo Bretholz, Oral History Transcript, USHMM Archives, RG-50.030*0038.
11. Ibid.
12. Ibid.
13. William J. Lowenberg, Oral History Interview, USHMM Archives RG-50.030*0139.
14. Irene Hasenberg Butter, Oral History Transcript, USHMM Archives, RG-50.155*0001, Acc. 1993. A. 0089.
15. Leo Bretholz.

Chapter 3. Worked to Death

1. Siegfried Halbreich, "Gross-Rosen," USHMM, n.d., <http://www.ushmm.org/wlc/media_oi.php?lang=en&ModuleId=10005454&MediaId=1215> (December 5, 2008).
2. Irene Hasenberg Butter, interview September 22, 1986, *Voice/Vision Holocaust Survivor Oral History Archive*, n.d., <http://holocaust.umd.umich.edu/butter/section010.html> (December 6, 2008).
3. Ibid., section 011.
4. Samuel Offen, interview December 27, 1981, *Voice/Vision Holocaust Survivor Oral History Archive*, n.d., <http://holocaust.umd.umich.edu/offens/section021.html> (December 3, 2008).
5. Marton Adler, interview July 13, 1989, *Voice/Vision Holocaust Survivor Oral History Archive*, n.d., <http://holocaust.umd.umich.edu/adler/section015.html> (December 3, 2008).
6. Paul Molnar, interview July 24, 2002, *Voice/Vision Holocaust Survivor Oral History Archive*, n.d., <http://holocaust.umd.umich.edu/interview.php?D=molnar&section=17> (December 3, 2008).
7. Sam Seltzer, interview November 29, 1982, *Voice/Vision Holocaust Survivor Oral History Archive*, n.d., <http://holocaust.umd.umich.edu/seltzer/section012.html> (December 3, 2008).
8. David Bergman, Oral History Transcript, USHMM Archives, RG-50.030.0020.
9. David Kahan, interview August 14, 1995, *Voice/Vision Holocaust Survivor Oral History Archive*, n.d., <http://holocaust.umd.umich.edu/kahan/section010.html> (December 3, 2008).
10. Hannah Fisk, interview January 24, 1983, *Voice/Vision Holocaust Survivor Oral History Archive*, n.d., <http://holocaust.umd.umich.edu/interview.php?D=fisk&section=13> (December 3, 2008).
11. Madeline Deutsch, Oral History Transcript, USHMM Archives, RG-50.549.01*0060.
12. Marton Adler.
13. Abraham Malach, Oral History Transcript, USHMM Archives, RG-50.030*0144.
14. David Kahan.
15. Ibid.

CHAPTER NOTES

16. Harry Prow, interview June 30, 1982, *Voice/Vision Holocaust Survivor Oral History Archive*, n.d., <http://holocaust.umd.umich.edu/interview.php?D=prow&section=22> (December 3, 2008).
17. Ibid.
18. David Kahan.
19. Paul Molnar.
20. From the Austrian court files in the trial of Dr. Guido Schmidt et al. as published in the *Wiener Arbeiterzeitung* from September 20, 1945, <http://www.jewishgen.org/ForgottenCamps/Camps/MauthausenEng.html> (December 5, 2008).
21. Fred Ferber, interview September 11, 2001, *Voice/Vision Holocaust Survivor Oral History Archive*, n.d., <http://holocaust.umd.umich.edu/ferberf/section020.html> (December 3, 2008).
22. Noemi Engel Ebenstein, interview July 22, 1996, *Voice/Vision Holocaust Survivor Oral History Archive*, n.d., <http://holocaust.umd.umich.edu/ebenstein/section016.html> (December 3, 2008).
23. Martin S. cited in Joshua M. Greene and Shiva Kumar, eds., *Witness: Voices from the Holocaust* (New York: Free Press, 2000), pp. 133–134.
24. Bernard Klein, interview May 23, 1984, *Voice/Vision Holocaust Survivor Oral History Archive*, n.d., <http://holocaust.umd.umich.edu/klein/section026.html> (December 3, 2008).

Chapter 4. The Death Camps

1. Robert Wagemann, "Euthanasia Program," USHMM, n.d., <http://www.ushmm.org/wlc/media_oi.php?lang=en&ModuleId=10005200&MediaId=1208> (December 5, 2008).
2. Viktor Brack, "Testimony," in *Trials of War Criminals Before the Nuremberg Military Tribunals*, Washington, D.C.: U.S. Government Printing Office, 1949–1953, vol. 1, pp. 876–886. Excerpts in <http://www.nizkor.org/ftp.cgi/places/germany/euthanasia/ftp.py?places/germany/euthanasia//brack.002> (December 20, 2008).
3. Ibid.
4. Ibid.
5. Testimony of gas-van driver Walter Burmeister, "Shofar FTP Archive Files: Camps/Chelmno//Burmeister-Testimony/Kulmhof," *Nizkor Project*, © 1991–2009, <www.nizkor.org/ftp.cgi/camps/chelmno/ftp.py?camps/chelmno//burmeister-testimony.kulmhof> (November 22, 2008).

6. Transcript of the Shoah interview with Simon Srebnik, translation by Sarah Lippincott, August 2008, <http://resources.ushmm.org/intermedia/film_video/spielberg_archive/transcript/RG60_5024/D8A39DB5-DE4C-419D-B650-5F3D448BF2EC.pdf> (December 15, 2008).
7. Jakub Lapides, "Jakub Lapides," USHMM, n.d., <http://www.ushmm.org/wlc/article.php?lang=en&ModuleId=10007291> (October 8, 2008).
8. "Chelmno," USHMM, May 4, 2009, <http://www.ushmm.org/wlc/article.php?lang=en&ModuleId=10005194> (April 14, 2009).
9. Testimony of Kurt Gersten, Nuremberg Tribunal PS 1553, cited in Alexander Kimel, "The Belzec Death Camp," *Holocaust Understanding and Prevention: Online Holocaust Magazine*, n.d., <http://kimel.net/belzec.html> (December 10, 2008).
10. Ibid.
11. Ibid.
12. Chaim Hirszman, cited in *Belzek Camp History*, 2005, <http://www.deathcamps.org/belzec/belzec.html> (December 12, 2008).
13. "Belzec," USHMM, May 4, 2009, <http://www.ushmm.org/wlc/article.php?lang=en&ModuleId=10005191> (December 15, 2008).
14. Thomas Blatt, *Interview by USC Shoah Foundation Institute for Visual History and Education, University of Southern California*, (Brooklyn, New York, 1995), interview code 1873, tape 4, segments 26, 30, 31, time code 03:30.
15. Tomasz Blatt, "Tomasz (Toivi) Blatt," USHMM, n.d., <http://www.ushmm.org/wlc/media_oi.php?lang=en&ModuleId=10006539&MediaId=4451> (December 3, 2008).
16. Ada Lichtmann, Yad Vashem Archives 0-3/1291, p. 18, cited in *Operation Reinhard: The Extermination Camps of Belzec, Sobibor and Treblinka*, 2009, <http://www.jewishvirtuallibrary.org/jsource/Holocaust/reinhard.html#4> (December 4, 2008).
17. Aharon Weiss, ed., "'Operation Reinhard': Extermination Camps of Belzec, Sobibor and Treblinka," The Nizkor Project, © 1991–2009, <http://nizkor.org/ftp.cgi/camps/ftp.py?camps//aktion.reinhard/yvs16.08> (June 29, 2009).
18. Ibid.
19. Nechamay Epstein, Yad Vashem Archives, 0.36/50.
20. Abraham Lewent, Oral History Transcript, USHMM Archives, RG-50.030*0130.

CHAPTER NOTES

21. Figures taken from several pages of *Holocaust Encyclopedia*: "Lublin/Majdanek Concentration Camp System: Areas of Research," USHMM, May 4, 2009, <http://www.ushmm.org/wlc/article.php?lang=en&ModuleId=10007299>; "Chelmno," <http://www.ushmm.org/wlc/article.php?lang=en&ModuleId=10005194>; "Belzec," <http://www.ushmm.org/wlc/article.php?lang=en&ModuleId=10005191>; "Sobibor," <http://www.ushmm.org/wlc/article.php?lang=en&ModuleId=10005192>; "Treblinka," <http://www.ushmm.org/wlc/article.php?lang=en&ModuleId=10005193>; "Auschwitz," <http://www.ushmm.org/wlc/article.php?lang=en&ModuleId=10005189> (April 12, 2009).

Chapter 5. Auschwitz

1. David Bergman, Oral History Transcript, USHMM Archives, RG-50.030*0020.
2. Kate Bernath, Oral History Transcript, USHMM Archives, RG-50.030.0023.
3. Helen Lebowitz Goldkind, Oral History Transcript, USHMM Archives, RG-50.233*0036.
4. Leo Schneiderman, Oral History Transcript, USHMM Archives, RG-50.030*0205.
5. Rudolf Franz Ferdinand Hoess, "Affidavit, 5 April 1946," in *Trial of the Major War Criminals Before the International Tribunal, Nuremberg, 14 November 1945–1 October 1946* (Nuremberg: Secretariat of the International Military Tribunal, 1949), Doc. 3868PS, vol. 33, 27579.
6. Ibid.
7. Ibid.
8. Abraham Malach, Oral History transcript, USHMM Archives, RG-50.030*0144.
9. David Bergman.
10. Fritzie Weiss Fritzshall, Oral History Transcript, USHMM Archives, RG-50.030*0075.
11. Edgar Krasa, Oral History Transcript, USHMM Archives, RG-50.030.0478.
12. Ibid.
13. Carola Steinhardt, Oral History Transcript, USHMM Archives, RG-50.030*0368.
14. Edgar Krasa.

15. Ruth Webber, Oral History Transcript, USHMM Archives, RG-50. 155*0007; Acc. 1993.H.089.
16. Eva Mozes, cited in Lucette Matalon Lagnado and Sheila Cohn Dekel, *Children of the Flames: Dr. Josef Mengele and the Untold Story of the Twins of Auschwitz* (New York: William Morrow and Company, 1991), p. 64.
17. Hedvah and Leah Stern, cited in Lagnado and Dekel, p. 66.
18. "Auschwitz," USHMM, May 4, 2009, <http://www.ushmm.org/wlc/article.php?ModuleId=10005189> (December 4, 2008).

Chapter 6. After the Camps

1. Thomas Blatt, *Interview by USC Shoah Foundation Institute for Visual History and Education, University of Southern California* (Brooklyn, New York, 1995), interview code 1873, tape 4, segments 26, 30, 31, time code 03:30.
2. Kalman Teigman's testimony at the Adolf Eichmann trial, cited in "Treblinka Death Camp Revolt," Holocaust Education and Archive Research Team, 2009, <http://www.holocaustresearchproject.org/ar/treblinka/revolt.html> (November 12, 2008).
3. Anna Heilmann, interviewed October 14, 1985, in *Women of Valor: Partisans and Resistance Fighters* <http://www3.sympatico.ca/mighty1/valor/anna1.htm> (November 6, 2008).
4. Fritzie Weiss Fritzshall, Oral History Transcript, USHMM Archives, RG-50.030*0075.
5. Lilly Appelbaum Malnik, "Death Marches," 1990 interview, USHMM, n.d., <http://www.ushmm.org/wlc/media_oi.php?lang=en&ModuleId=10005162&MediaId=1171> (December 15, 2008).
6. Ibid.
7. Fritzie Weiss.
8. Lily Mazur Margules, "Death Marches," 1990 interview, USHMM, n.d., <http://www.ushmm.org/wlc/media_oi.php?lang=en&ModuleId=10005162&MediaId=1172> (December 15, 2008).
9. Sam Itzkowitz, "Death Marches," 1991 interview, USHMM, n.d., <http://www.ushmm.org/wlc/media_oi.php?lang=en&ModuleId=10005162&MediaId=1216> (December 15, 2008).
10. Fritzie Weiss.

CHAPTER NOTES

11. Harry J. Herder, Jr., "The Liberation of Buchenwald," *Remember.org*, n.d., <http://remember.org/witness/herder.html> (April 3, 2009).
12. Ibid.
13. Ibid.
14. Bela Braver, in Yehudit Kleiman and Nina Springer-Aharoni, eds., *The Anguish of Liberation, Testimonies from 1954* (Jerusalem: Yad Vashem, 1995), p. 19.
15. Eva Braun, in Kleiman and Springer-Aharoni, p. 19.
16. Fela Warschau, "Displaced Persons," 1995 interview, USHMM, n.d., <http://www.ushmm.org/wlc/media_oi.php?lang=en&ModuleId=10005462&MediaId=3282> (December 15, 2008).
17. Thomas Buergenthal, "Displaced Persons," USHMM, n.d., <http://www.ushmm.org/wlc/media_oi.php?lang=en&ModuleId=10005462&MediaId=2491> (December 15, 2008).
18. Irene Hasenberg Butter, interview September 22, 1986, *Voice/Vision Holocaust Survivor Oral History Archive*, n.d., <http://holocaust.umd.umich.edu/butter/section008.html> (December 8, 2008).
19. Ellen Levi, cited in Deborah Dwork, *Children with a Star: Jewish Youth in Nazi Europe* (New Haven, Conn.: Yale University Press, 1991), p. 249.
20. Cited in Adam Phillips, "An Auschwitz Survivor Remembers," *Voice of America News*, January 27, 2005, <http://www.voanews.com/english/archive/2005-01/2005-01-27-voa44.cfm> (December 15, 2008).
21. Alice Lok Cahana, *Women Artists of the American West*, n.d., <http://www.cla.purdue.edu/WAAW/Ressler/artists/cahanastat.html> (November 18, 2008).

GLOSSARY

Allies—Countries that fought against Germany, Japan, and Italy during World War II. The Allied countries were Great Britain, the United States, the Soviet Union, and twenty-three other countries.

antisemitism—Prejudice against Jews.

armistice—A truce between warring parties agreeing to stop the fighting.

crematorium (plural, crematoria)—Facility in which the bodies of people who had been killed in gas chambers were burned. The term was often used to refer to a complex of facilities that included gas chambers and ovens.

euthanasia—Usually the act of killing in a painless way to prevent a person from suffering. The term was used by Nazis as an excuse for deliberately killing certain people.

gendarme—A French policeman.

Gentile—A non-Jewish person.

Gestapo—The *Geheime Staatspolizei*, the State Secret Police of Nazi Germany.

kapo—Concentration camp inmate who has been given authority over some of the other inmates.

lager—Literally "a storehouse," the German name for a camp or a section of a camp such as a barrack.

Nazi—Member of, or pertaining to, the National Socialist German Workers' Party, a political organization based on principles of extreme nationalism, militarism, racism, and totalitarianism.

GLOSSARY

satellite camp—Smaller camp associated with a larger camp nearby.

Schutzstaffel (SS)—Literally "protection squad." The SS was originally a group that served as Hitler's personal bodyguards and became a military-like organization that provided staff for camp guards, police units, and some fighting units.

Sonderkommando ("special squad")—Group of inmates who removed items from victims who were killed in the camps and then disposed of their bodies.

Torah—Often translated as " written law," generally refers to the Five Books of Moses, or the books of the Hebrew Bible. A Torah scroll is written on parchment in a formal, traditional manner by a trained scribe. It is the holiest of the sacred writings in Judaism.

FURTHER READING

Boraks-Nemetz, Lilian and Irene N. Watts, eds. *Tapestry of Hope: Holocaust Writing for Young People*. Plattsburg, N.Y.: Tundra Books of Northern New York, 2003.

Gilbert, Martin. *The Boys: The Story of 732 Young Concentration Camp Survivors*. New York: Macmillan, 1998.

Gottfried, Ted. *Children of the Slaughter: Young People of the Holocaust*. Brookfield, Conn.: Twenty-First Century Books, 2001.

Jackson, Livia Bitton. *I Have Lived a Thousand Years: Growing up in the Holocaust*. New York: Simon & Schuster, 1999.

Shuter, Jane. *Life and Death in the Camps*. Chicago: Heinemann Library, 2003.

Warren, Andrea. *Surviving Hitler: A Boy in the Nazi Death Camps*. New York: HarperCollins, 2002.

Zapruder, Alexandra, ed. *Salvaged Pages: Young Writers' Diaries of the Holocaust*. New Haven, Conn.: Yale University Press, 2002.

INTERNET ADDRESSES

United States Holocaust Memorial Museum
 <http://www.ushmm.org/>

University of Southern California Shoah Foundation Institute
 <http://college.usc.edu/vhi/>

Yad Vashem, The Holocaust Martyrs'
 and Heroes' Remembrance Authority
 <http://www.yadvashem.org.il/>

INDEX

A
Adler, Marton, 45, 49–50
antisemitism, 13–15, 27
Appelbaum, Lilly, 96–98
Auschwitz
    crematoria, 7
    death march, 95–98
    death statistics, 77, 92
    described, 30, 78–81
    establishment of, 7, 22, 63, 78
    gas chambers, 7, 9, 78, 81, 91
    as labor camp, 78, 81, 85–87, 91–92, 95
    liberation of, 92, 95, 104–105
    medical experimentation, 90–91
    rebellion, 9, 93, 94, 109
    selection process, 78–85, 89–90
Autobahn, 47

B
Belzec, 63, 67–71, 77, 95
Bergen-Belsen, 11–12, 43, 105
Bergman, David, 47, 78–79, 83–84
Bernath, Kate, 79
Blatt, Thomas, 71–72, 93
Brack, Viktor, 60–62
Braun, Eva, 104–105
Braver, Bela, 104
Bretholz, Leo, 35–38, 41
Buchenwald, 18, 21, 101–103
Buergenthal, Thomas, 106
Burmeister, Walter, 64–65

C
Chelmno, 63–67, 77, 95
collaboration, 32
concentration camps. *See also* specific camps.
    establishment of, 13
    liberation of, 100–106
    overview, 18–21
    as punishment, 15, 19
    purpose, 15, 25

D
Dachau, 18–20, 45, 51, 99–100
dead, statistics, 12, 77, 92
death camps, 25, 63–64. *See also* specific camps.
death marches, 92, 95–100
deportations, 25, 32–33, 40–41, 63, 66–67, 73, 75
Deutsch, Madeline, 48–49
disease, 32, 44, 68, 75, 96, 105
displaced persons (DP) camps, 105–106
Dora, 45, 49–50, 51–53
Drancy, 33–38, 41

E
Einsatzgruppen (killing squads), 25
Epstein, Hedy, 18–19
Epstein, Nechamah, 75–77

F
Feigl, Peter, 27–30
Ferber, Fred, 55–57

"final solution," 7, 23–25, 33, 63, 75, 81
Fisk, Hannah, 48
Flossenbürg, 18
forced labor camps. *See also* specific camps.
    building, 42
    children, young in, 50, 57–58
    death in, 46, 47, 49–57
    described, 23, 25, 43–44
    starvation in, 42, 50–51
    work types, 45–50
France, 27–33

G

Gabersdorf, 48
gas vans, 64–65, 66
Gehsperre Aktion, 66–67
Gerstein, Kurt, 67–71
Gestapo, 14–15, 23–24
ghettos, 12, 24–25, 27, 44, 63, 64, 66, 71, 73
Gordon, Alexander, 23–24
Gross-Rosen, 42–43, 47, 48
Grynszpan, Herschel, 15
Guben, 9–11
Gurs, 29–30, 32

H

Haas, Theodore, 19–20
Halbreich, Siegfried, 42
Hasenberg, Irene, 40–41, 42–43
Heilmann, Anna, 94
Herder, Harry, 101–103
Himmler, Heinrich, 25, 27, 55, 63, 75, 92, 95
Hitler, Adolf, 7, 13, 14, 15, 59
Höss, Rudolf, 81–83

I

Itzkowitz, Sam, 99–100

K

Kahan, David, 47–48, 50–51, 53–54
Klein, Bernard, 58
Koenig, Ernest, 33–35
Krasa, Edgar, 85–86, 87
Kristallnacht (Night of Broken Glass), 15–18, 19, 20
Kutner, Leo, 22–23

L

Lang, Eva, 31–32
Lapides, Jakub, 66–67
Lebowitz, Helen, 79–80
Lichtmann, Ada, 73
Liebmann, Max, 32
Lok, Alice, 7–12, 109
Lowenberg, William, 38–40
Lowenthal, Laurie, 16–18

M

Majdanek, 63, 75–77, 91, 95
Malach, Abraham, 50, 82–83
Mauthausen, 18, 23, 54–57
Mazur, Lily, 98–99
Mengele, Josef, 82–83, 90–92
Molnar, Paul, 45–46, 54
Müldorf, 48, 50–51, 53–54

N

Nazi brutality
    beatings, 78–80
    deception, 42–43, 68, 73–74, 82, 85

dehumanization, 38, 55, 58, 68, 85–89
intimidation, 15, 20, 21, 43
murder, 16–18, 20, 21, 25, 44, 49, 55, 95–101
theft, 21, 70, 72, 73
torture, 15, 20, 21, 43, 54, 57, 74, 90–92
vandalism, 15–18
Nazi Party, 13

O
Operation Reinhard, 63–64, 71, 73

P
Peterswaldan, 48–49
prisoner-of-war (POW) camps, 21
Prow, Harry, 51–53
psychological effects, 106–109

R
Rath, Ernst vom, 15
refugee camps, 27–33
Reichenbach, 47
Rivesaltes, 30–32, 35, 38
Rosenfeld, Ursula, 20–21

S
Sachsenhausen, 18, 42
Schneiderman, Leo, 80–81
Seltzer, Sam, 47
Sobibor, 63, 71–73, 77, 93, 95
Sonderkommando, 66, 94, 109
SS (*Schutzstaffel*)
    beatings, 19, 22, 43, 54
    deception, 68, 73
    intimidation by, 66, 84, 85, 87
    murder, 44, 55, 67–70
    in selection process, 24, 50, 81–82
Starachowice, 50
starvation, 12, 20, 32, 36, 42, 51, 75, 96
Steinhardt, Carola, 86–87
Stern, Hedvah, Leah, 90
Stutthof, 22–23, 98–99

T
Teigman, Kalman, 93–94
T4 euthanasia program, 59–64
transit camps, 27, 33–41
Treblinka, 63, 73–75, 77, 81, 93–95

W
Wagemann, Robert, 59–60
Warschau, Fela, 105–106
Webber, Ruth, 89–90
Weiss, Fritzie, 84–85, 95–96, 98, 100
Westerbork, 33, 38–41, 43
World War II, 21–23

Z
Zieres, Franz, 54–55